To Don,

Two road diverged in a wood, and I,
I took the one less traveled by,
And that has made all the difference,
Robert Frost

Chuck Luttrell

Vishnu Temple Press
PO Box 30821
Flagstaff AZ 86003
(928) 556 0742
www.vishnutemplepress.com

The Making of a Ranger
A Life in the Great Outdoors

by

Chuck Luttrell

Vishnu Temple Press
Flagstaff, Arizona

Contents

Introduction

I'm sitting warm and comfortable in my old wingback chair in front of a flickering fire in the fireplace. In the next room I can hear the murmur of the television and Eileen, my wife, moving about in the kitchen. It's the eve following Thanksgiving and the holiday has put me in a reflective mood. I have reached the midpoint of my life and, as I take stock, I count myself a most fortunate man. I'm doing what I want to do. I've lived my dreams, though not always as I had originally planned, and I've achieved my goals.

Early in life I knew that I wanted a life of excitement, adventure, and freedom that exists only in the open air. I wanted life without walls. I needed freedom from clocks, schedules, quotas, and repetition. A ranger career seemed to offer all of that and so it was the path I chose. However, this career choice was made before I met and married Eileen. Without consideration for the aspirations and goals of a future wife, I had planned my life. Eileen's dream of becoming a lawyer did not immediately fit into my dream of becoming a ranger. Hence, my life story is about the meshing of two completely different personalities into a comfortable, workable compromise.

The faint sound of rain pattering against the window draws my thoughts away from the past. I hear the loud ticking of the cuckoo clock. I see small fingers of flame dance around the logs in the fireplace. In his chair next to me, William Wallace, my loyal gray tabby, lies curled in sleep. Okay, so I'm not sitting beside my campfire with the collar of my sheepskin coat turned up to protect me from wind and rain. But my life is a satisfactory combination of outdoor activity–my job–and indoor tranquility–my home.

I look around this room and see old college textbooks; a painting of Mount Trumbull hangs over the fireplace; on the wall next to the cuckoo clock there's a ranger's Smokey the Bear campaign hat—all reminders, souvenirs of my amazing life. I didn't miss a thing. I've had it all and then some.

The hypnotic ticking of the clock and dancing flames in the fireplace take me back again to a time many years ago in a place half a continent away. I remember a night long ago spent fighting a wildfire. I feel the claustrophobic darkness. I see little tongues of flame peek out under a fallen log. I imagine nearby silhouetted tree trunks swaying crazily and I can almost smell the smoke washing over me in waves. One moment the air is clean and cool; the next hot and choking.

I'm in the Appalachian Mountains paired up with another young ranger as a sawyer and swamper. As we cut a narrow slot through thickets of brush and saplings I hear somewhere below us the rest of the crew chopping and scratching away the undergrowth. I'm tired. I feel the burning ache of muscle as I heft the saw and wonder if I can make it through the night.

Then suddenly, as only thoughts or dreams can do, I'm transported to another time and place. Now I'm on a mountain in Utah. A big log, a foot and a half in diameter, is crashing down on me. With no way to escape I leap straight up. The log catches me on the shins and carries me over a precipice. Miraculously the giant rolling pin shoots under me and careens on down the mountain. Catlike, I've just used up one of my nine lives.

A low rumble of thunder brings me back to my cozy living room. William Wallace still sleeps and Eileen has finished her work in the kitchen. Rain is silently washing down the windows. I'm glad I'm not on a mountainside battling a wildfire, but I'm also glad I have this and many more exciting memories.

I achieved my goal. I became a ranger, but I never anticipated the twists and turns, the choices and challenges along the way. Of hair-raising outdoor adventures, I've had my share.

- 1 -

Destiny

I grew up in a middle class family in an ordinary small town—Boulder City, Nevada. Loved and raised on old-fashioned textbook values, everything about my life was normal except for my summers on Grandma and Grandpa's ranch in Arizona.

At the end of each school term, my parents farmed my brother and me out to my mother's parents. As the time to go to the ranch approached, my brother Dave and I grew more and more excited. It wasn't just the fact that Grandma and Grandpa would spoil us. Life on the ranch was an adventure—like being transplanted into the exciting world of the old West. With fifty years of hindsight, I see clearly that it was my days on the ranch that have made all the difference—that shaped my destiny.

The Craig Ranch, once a working cattle operation, was, by the 1960s, one of the last homesteads on the Arizona Strip. We called it "the ranch" even though my grandparents lived in semi-retirement; cattle and horses no longer grazed their land. This real "magic kingdom" was situated in a remote part of Arizona, cut off from the rest of the state by the Grand Canyon. It was, and still is, a lonesome, unpopulated land. The homestead lay in the center of this wilderness in a high sage-covered valley at the toe of the north slope of Mount Trumbull and flanked on the east and west by piñon- and juniper-covered hills. It was a world unto itself. The ranch's only visible link to the outside was a narrow, one-lane, dusty—or muddy, depending on the season—road. The only neighbor within several dozen miles was a park ranger, John Riffey.

9

The RV Ranch headquarters, or more accurately Grandpa's place, was still part of an earlier time. The modest house may have had, if I'm generous, a footprint of 600 square feet. The pine board and batten structure had a covered front porch and a steep roof which created a cozy attic bedroom. This loft was the preferred quarters of visiting grandchildren and was accessed by a ladder-like set of stairs on the outside of the building.

The house was heated in the bitter cold winters by a large wood stove in the living and dining room. Meals were prepared on another wood stove in the kitchen. There was no electric power or phone or television. Several large windows provided daytime lighting and evening light came from kerosene lamps. The only indoor plumbing was a cold water faucet at the kitchen sink. The water—a thin, meager stream—came from barrels located on a little hill behind the house.

Also behind the house were a storage shed, a privy, and a cellar. The cool, dark cellar served as a pantry and housed provisions that could keep the ranch supplied for many weeks if necessary, and during snowbound winters it was often necessary. Near the kitchen back door was a shed, one end of which was filled with miscellaneous cast-offs. In the fall the other end was stacked to overflowing with firewood in preparation for the harsh winter weather.

A dozen steps north of the main house squatted an old 1930s-vintage trailer house which was used as guest quarters. Beyond that was a second dugout also used as guest accommodations. This dugout, or cellar, was a large 14 by 18-foot room with a fireplace. With earthen walls and a ceiling made of split cedar logs, the dugout was well insulated. It stayed cool in the summer and held in the fireplace's warmth in the winter.

Past the dugout were chicken coops and the barn. The barn bore no resemblance to the red structure pictured in my first grade reader. It was, instead, a long, shed-like building with pine slab walls and a corrugated tin roof. The first two bays were open on one side and served as garages in my time, but, in years past, had been livestock stalls. Next came the feed room and the saddle shop. Finally, at the far end of the building were two bays that housed the machine and blacksmith shops. Scattered down from the machine shop, nearly to the front gate, was a bone yard—the final resting place of the disassembled remains of dozens of old vehicles and machines. The ranch wasn't much to look at, especially if judged by the standards of material comfort and conveniences of modern city living, yet it was a place I longed to return to at the end of each school year.

Summer at the ranch meant baths only once a week, usually on Saturday night, and flapjacks for breakfast every morning. I can still see Grandma standing by the wood-burning cook stove flipping hot, fluffy flapjacks and my mouth waters when I remember the appetizing smell of sizzling bacon. But best of all were the card games played by lamp light on the big dining table every evening.

Life was lived at a slower, simpler pace. We got up early, but we went to bed early. There were no scheduled activities. Each day unfolded naturally. Chores that needed to be done, like feeding the chickens, gathering eggs, and bringing in fire wood were taken care of right after breakfast. It took a lot of fuel to keep that stove supplied. Bringing in the wood and stacking it in the wood-box was Dave's and my job.

After morning chores the day could go anywhere. Usually we would tag along with Grandpa while he went about his daily business, which might be gathering and cutting fire wood or a trip to Nixon Spring on the other side of Trumbull to haul drinking water. If we were really lucky, the day's work might involve one of the ranch's tractors.

At least once a week drinking water had to be hauled from Nixon Spring. The trip to the spring, six miles away, was one of my favorite chores. Elvis, the old 1952 Ford pickup, would be loaded with 50-gallon drums. Dave and I would sit atop these barrels and ride them like bucking broncos. At Nixon Spring, Grandpa would back the truck up to the large concrete water trough. A pipe dribbled cold, delicious water into the trough and Grandpa would attach a hose and begin filling the barrels.

This was a slow process, taking nearly an hour for each barrel. Grandpa would sit on the tailgate smoking his carefully rolled Bull Durham cigarette while Dave and I played in the water trough or explored the deep grass around the shore of the adjacent pond looking for frogs.

After water hauling came laundry day. Washing was done in an old-fashioned gasoline-powered washing machine and this was no day for idleness. All hands had to pitch in and, while I doubt that we were overly helpful, Dave and I did our best carrying buckets of water and tubs of wet clothing.

The big meal of the day was served at noon. When Grandma hollered, "Dinner!" from the front porch, we stopped whatever we were doing and hurried to the house. I don't remember much about the meals except that there were always plenty of beans and potatoes.

After dinner, Grandpa would settle down on the porch to take a nap and Dave and I would go off to play on our own. In our younger years we played in a tree house Grandpa had built in a big piñon. Remodeling this platform was a favorite activity. One day it was our secret club house and the next we turned it into a fort and, on occasion, we converted it into a crow's nest on the mast of our make-believe schooner. Sometimes we pretended to be soldiers. We would sneak around the ranch buildings looking for the enemy, who usually looked like Grandma.

As we grew older our afternoon play evolved into bolder more adventurous activities. Dave and I, along with our two dogs, would set off in some direction to explore. We would wander off, going no place in particular, examining each new discovery with the pure, fearless curiosity of childhood. Sometimes we planned our treks. We would pack a knap sack and strap on old army surplus canteens and head out. Grandpa would sit on the porch and, as he smoked a hand-rolled cigarette, he would ask, "Where are Lewis and Clark heading today?"

With hundreds of acres in the middle of thousands of square miles it would not have been unreasonable to expect kids brought up in town to be intimidated. But we weren't. In fact, its very frontier-like feeling made it all the more desirable. Dave and I ranged all over the ranch, climbing every peak and ridge, exploring wind-carved caves and hidden valleys.

While I tell all this with great fondness, the real point is how those days on the ranch shaped me. Living close to the earth surrounded by the beauty of the wild untamed land, where each day was governed by the weather and self motivation, I was being molded. And my grandfather was a great role model. He didn't hire a helper or go to the store to buy something that could be fixed. As I watched him repair a truck or tractor I was impressed by his hard work, toughness, and resourcefulness. He didn't measure success by wealth or possessions, but by intangibles like freedom, simplicity, and independence. He had had opportunities for a softer, easier life, but he chose the hard life of a rancher on the Arizona Strip. Toughness, self-reliance, and independence were all requirements for survival in that country and Grandpa, who possessed these traits in abundance, saw to it that these lessons were learned by my brother and me. You didn't cry around Grandpa and you had to figure things out for yourself. Long before I would make conscious decisions about my future, deep in my unconscious mind, my destiny was already being formed.

The ranch pointed me in a general direction, but it was Grandpa's friend and nearest neighbor, Ranger John Riffey, who fine-tuned my decision. He manned a ranger station about twenty-two miles south of Grandpa's ranch—near the rim of the Grand Canyon. Riffey, as we called him, was my grandfather's closest friend. At the time I didn't really understand the meaning of "park ranger." To me Riffey was just another rancher although I did recognize that his "ranch" was different. Dressed in twill work pants, plaid shirt, and a battered, sweat-stained, straw cowboy hat instead of a uniform, Riffey looked more like a cowboy than a ranger. The only thing I noticed that gave his identity away as a "G" man was the "For Official Use Only" markings on the doors of his old pickup truck. Riffey was, from my boyhood perspective, just part of the summers at the ranch. He appeared to do the same kind of things my grandpa did and there was nothing about his days that indicated he was working for anyone but himself. He appeared to be his own man.

For Christmas in the early 1960s, Riffey gave me a Park Service gray Penney's work shirt with one of his old uniform arrowhead patches sewn on the sleeve. I treasured that shirt, not because it was a ranger's shirt, but because it was a uniform shirt.

I didn't really think about my future in those days for I lived only in the present. But if I had given thought to the future I doubt I would have considered rangering, because I believed astronaut, fireman, or engineer were careers, but what Riffey did was a lifestyle—just how you lived.

Some years later, around my sophomore year of high school, I started having my first serious thoughts about my future and a career. I had toyed with several ideas, but for the most part I was adrift. I thought I might like to be a naval architect, but I lacked the commitment to apply myself to the requisite study of mathematics. As my high school senior year approached, I began to feel pressure to select a direction, but what direction?

Then quite by accident the direction I was seeking emerged. It had been there all along waiting in my subconscious. One day, my brother Dave announced that he and his best friend were going to be park rangers. Park ranger! That was it! It was an epiphany. Working outdoors in the wilds doing whatever it was that Riffey did all day was exactly what I wanted to do. With no deeper thought than, that sounds fun, I selected my life's work. I wish I could say I carefully considered all my options, did some research, but I didn't. Something inside clicked and that was it.

Interestingly, everything I knew about the life of a park ranger was wrong. My understanding was based on John Riffey who was, by the time I knew him, an anomaly in the Park Service. His way of rangering was from a bygone era. The job of modern park rangers had already evolved to meet a changing world. But I didn't know this. To me ranger meant a life lived outdoors, freedom, and adventure. The job was to take care of the land, fight forest fires, and greet the visitors. I would become a park ranger.

- *2* -

Hard Work and Disappointment

I always knew that I would go to college. Mom and Dad had it so deeply ingrained in me that I thought it was the automatic next step after high school. However, once I decided to become a ranger, college was no longer simply a moral obligation, but an absolute necessity. For me, it was sort of like getting your union card—it was something a ranger must have.

I ended up going to the University of Nevada, Las Vegas (UNLV), and the University of Nevada, Reno (UNR), but these weren't my first choice. I wanted to go to Colorado State at Fort Collins, Colorado, because it was known as the "ranger factory," and also because my role model, John Riffey, had gone there. As it turned out however, I couldn't afford Colorado State.

During my first two years of college at UNLV I lived at home. This was both convenient and helped cut expenses, but UNLV didn't offer the degree program I needed. In the fall of 1977, I transferred to UNR and began my study of "Renewable Natural Resources." Once I was with other students with my same interests, a whole new world opened up for me. I learned that the National Park Service hired summer help—"seasonals." Seasonal ranger! That sounded perfect. But to be sure of getting a summer job I applied for every job listed: ranger, firefighter, forestry technician, and maintenance worker.

Imagine my disappointment when, by May, I had not been offered a single job. Each day in class I would listen to my fellow students discussing their job offers and summer plans. It appeared I would be going back to construction work but, just days before the

15

semester was over, Lake Mead National Recreation Area called. They wanted to know if I would take a laborer job at Willow Beach, a small marina and campground located on the Colorado River, down stream from Hoover Dam. I jumped at the opportunity. Sure, it wasn't exactly how I planned to begin my career, but it was a start.

In the summertime Willow Beach is Hell's furnace. By July, the daytime highs often passed 120°. On hot days, the clear water of the Colorado River looked inviting, but I soon learned that it was actually cold, very cold. Because the water came from the deep, cold bottom of Lake Mead, it was a teeth-chattering 54 degrees at Willow Beach. There was no such thing as a refreshing dip in the river.

My job was pure, unchallenging routine, but I loved it. Every day in the morning and again in the afternoon, I cleaned seventy-two toilets and urinals. I picked up trash along the beaches and roads, emptied garbage cans, pruned and irrigated the oleanders and trees of the campground. Day after day it was the same, hot, hard, and sometimes dirty work. I saw Willow Beach as my personal responsibility and I made sure it was neat and clean.

Part of our routine was to pick up the roadside litter along the 4-mile access road every Monday morning. The first time out on this job I rode in the cab of our Dodge pickup with the local maintenance man. We would drive along slowly, stop at each piece of paper or can, get out, pick it up, get back in, and go. Too slow! My impatience soon prompted a change. I began riding on the back bumper to speed things up. Soon however, this developed into a competition to see how fast we could police the four miles. By the end of summer the truck never stopped. I would jump off, run and scoop up the offending litter, run back and jump onto the truck. Even in those days of more relaxed rules, I know our boss would have had a fit if he had known what we were doing. We were, however, fast and efficient. He never questioned how we did it.

It was during that first summer that I saw what modern rangers did. When I met District Ranger Bill Sherman, his actions convinced me that here was a worthy role model. He was a resourceful outdoorsman, much like the early rangers of the National Park Service.

Because of the increasing demands on the Park Service, new rangers were becoming more and more single-function servants. But here and there were some holdouts like Bill, who believed emptying a trash can wasn't beneath them, giving a nature program to a group of visitors wasn't someone else's job, and monitoring the wilderness wasn't a forgotten function.

One day while irrigating oleanders in the upper camp ground, I saw smoke coming from a rear compartment of a camp trailer. I immediately radioed the ranger station. Next I pounded on the trailer door. No answer. The door was unlocked so I stepped inside the smoke-filled room, called out, listened for an answer and then, choking on fumes, backed out.

That's when Bill arrived with the 100-gallon pumper trailer in tow. As I watched, he yanked open the rear compartment where an overheated electric generator had started the fire. Quickly he quenched the flames with a stream of water from the pumper. Up to that point, his actions were routine, what any ranger would do. It was what happened next that impressed me. Bill opened the camp trailer's door and where I had backed out, he plunged in. A few seconds later, he emerged with a little dog in his arms.

That first summer passed quickly and I earned the reputation of being a good hand. I was anxious to return to school, because I now felt like a proud veteran. I was certain I would fit in with all the other upperclassmen. But, back in the academic world, I soon found out my summer as a laborer was completely discounted. Apparently, if you hadn't counted bugs or measured weeds, you hadn't had a meaningful experience.

Year Two at Reno went by much as the first had, but with one important difference. A middle-aged man who had returned to school for a career change, gave me some useful advice. He said, "Chuck, you've got to build a resumé. You have to make yourself hireable." He was a volunteer fireman and he suggested that in order to gain experience, I should join a volunteer fire department.

Intent on getting on the right track, I joined the Truckee Meadows Fire Protection District as an auxiliary firefighter in the fall of

1978. Truckee Meadows was the fire department for Washoe County. I was issued turnout gear, a radio, a training schedule, and told to go to any fires the Truckee, Mayberry or Sun Valley Engine Companies were dispatched to.

It's hard to imagine now that they would turn somebody as green as I was loose at a fire scene but, a month after I signed on, I got my first big fire. An old dairy barn was ablaze. Hundred-foot flames lit up the night sky. I had yet to attend any real training and I didn't know what to do. I parked several hundred yards away from the fire on an old dirt lane leading up to the barn and raced up the hill. Seeing a figure near one of the fire engines I approached and asked what I should do. "Don't ask me, go ask the Chief!" he shouted over the drone of the engine's pump.

I looked around. Where was the Chief? What should I do? I stepped away from the pumper. I suddenly noticed that it was cold, very cold. Next to the fire engine, the heat from the truck and the bright halogen lights created a small microclimate but, back out in the dark, it was well below freezing. As I stood there wondering what to do next, another new auxiliary fireman ran by and signaled me to follow. Talk about the blind leading the blind!

Fire was quickly consuming the barn (a huge, wooden structure that had stood empty on a small hill overlooking Reno for years) and it was collapsing in upon itself. The other new man and I found the Chief and he told us to man the 2½-inch hose. The regular paid firemen that had been on the hose were going back to the engine to warm up. Feeling like real firefighters with an important assignment, the two of us began spraying a big stream onto the fire. Soon the building fell down and was nothing more than a pile of burning lumber. We continued to work the powerful stream of water back and forth over the debris. Clouds of smoke and steam billowed up. It was like standing in a cloud. We couldn't see more than a few feet in any direction. The only indication that the fire still burned was the dull orange glow in front of us.

We sprayed right and left, up and down. It was exciting. It was fun. We were real firemen doing what real firemen do.

A muffled shout came from somewhere in front of us. It sounded far away and I couldn't make out the words over the roar of our big nozzle. Then, suddenly, out of the cloud of steam and smoke came an ice-encrusted, mad as hell firefighter. "You idiots!" he yelled. "Didn't you hear me? You're soaking us!"

How could that be? We were putting out the fire, not spraying anyone. Were there firemen in the fire?

The iceman leaned forward and hissed, "We're on the other side. Your stream is going over the fire."

I apologized, but I'm sure the sincerity of my apology was questioned because of the big grin on my face.

During my eight months with the Truckee Meadows, I must say I gathered very little training or experience for my résumé, but it was exciting and I did get introduced to one tragic but all to common fact of life for emergency workers—death.

I had seen death before when my grandfather died. While it was a terrible time, it was expected and somehow less jarring. My first encounter with a traumatic death, even that of a stranger bothered me for several days. No matter what I was doing—walking to class, reading a textbook, or cleaning my room—I would see that charred, disfigured body.

It happened when I was called to a mobile home fire. By the time the first fire engine arrived on the scene, the trailer was fully engulfed in flames. Our attack was defensive, that is, we remained on the outside and directed the water streams into the trailer. After the fire was knocked down, another fireman and I were told to take a hose in through the front door and finish mopping up the flames.

Inside everything was black, charred, and lay scattered about in indiscernible mounds. Slowly we worked our way through the room, spraying water, digging through and turning over the debris to root out the last of the fire.

We had been inside about ten minutes when the Engine Captain came in behind us. Immediately he announced he had found a body. I turned around and there right by the door, where we had entered was a black lump. I looked closer and, with rising horror, I made out the form of what was once a human being. It had no human characteristics left other than in the gross shape. It looked like a frankfurter roasted on a stick over a campfire—black on the outside and split open. The sight was overwhelming, but more alarming was the realization that when we had entered the room we must have stepped on it. The thought almost made me sick. For several days after the incident I couldn't get it out of my mind.

In time I would learn how to cope better. I would learn never to look at the eyes, not to make it a person. Think of it only as a body, so much tissue and bone, nothing more. Even then sometimes it's hard. Nobody gets used to it.

During the spring semester of my senior year I was hit with another disappointment. My student advisor called me into his office and explained that, in spite of the fact that I had enough credits to graduate, not all of my transfer classes from UNLV counted. I would have to return for the fall semester. It was heartbreaking news.

That spring, just as I had done before, I applied for ranger positions at a number of national parks. I also, just for back up, put in an application at Lake Mead for laborer. And, as before, I received no job offers until at the last minute when Lake Mead called. I was disappointed at not getting a ranger job, especially since I now had firefighter experience. But at least I was involved with the National Park Service.

In the fall of 1979, after my second summer at Willow Beach, I returned to Reno for my final semester and I graduated that December. I had no job prospects, yet my optimism as a freshly minted college graduate couldn't be dampened by the "real world." I was on my way up. I didn't realize that a bumpy road full of twists and turns lay ahead.

- 3 -

Distracted

I met Eileen O'Neill less than a year before I graduated when she came to my college dorm with a friend to visit my roommate. The first time I saw her dark hair, brown eyes, and petite figure, I was attracted. To say I fell in love at first sight is perhaps an overstatement, but Eileen definitely captured my attention.

During my first years at UNR I had been too busy and too focused on my goal for girls. But with only a month before graduation in December the pressure was off. I could think about girls and the girl I thought about was Eileen. I finally got my courage up and asked her out on a date.

In retrospect I have no idea why she ever agreed to go out with me and then accepted a second invitation, because I was definitely no Romeo. With little experience I felt like a hayseed. I was clumsy in dating protocol and struggled to make interesting conversation. Nevertheless, she didn't turn away and I was soon falling in love.

Eileen is Native American and grew up in the small community of Lovelock in central Nevada. Technically her family lived on a Piute reservation, but the place looked like any small town in America. In a funny kind of way, I was secretly disappointed because it didn't look like what I had imagined as an Indian village.

They say opposites attract and that is the only way to explain our mutual attraction. No two people could be more opposite than the two of us. I'm a country boy at heart and she is a city girl. I'm noisy and she is quiet. She is prim and proper and I'm, well let's say, a little less concerned about appearance and social issues. She is deliberate in her thinking and I operate about half the time on gut instinct, which I should add, is often wrong. And, what I am most grateful for, she is grace under pressure. She is calm, steady, and rock solid in times of trial when I tend to get excited and emotional.

However, I knew none of this then. What I saw was a beautiful woman who was smart, kind, and fun to be around. Somehow I knew this was the love of my life and I never questioned how little I knew about her or how improbable our prospects together were.

After graduation, I returned home for the Christmas holiday. I had met Eileen's parents and, because I wanted my parents to meet Eileen, I invited her to come to Boulder City for a week in January. When I think back now to those days what amazes me is what happened next. Without prior planning or thought, I proposed. I wasn't romantic, certainly I was not on bended knee, when I said, "Will you marry me?" What is even more improbable, this woman who barely knew me and could have no possible idea what a future with me would be, said yes.

Eileen returned to UNR in January and I soon followed her. I roomed with a friend and got a job on a construction crew. Every day I worked out on a demolition crew and every evening I walked the two miles from the place where I was staying to the university dorm to visit Eileen. With the lack of sleep and regular meals, it was no wonder that in March I came down with mononucleosis. Before I knew what was happening, I was in the hospital and really sick. After several days in St. Mary's Hospital, my dad brought me back home. For the next few weeks I just lay around the house too sick to do anything.

As in the previous two years, I had applied for summer seasonal work with the Park Service. In April, Lake Mead called. This time they offered me a laborer job at Cottonwood Cove and I accepted. But, when my doctor learned I planned to return to work at the end of May he said, "No way."

However, never underestimate the power of youth and determination. And on the appointed day I stepped—still shaky but able to stand on my own two feet—into the maintenance shop at Cottonwood Cove.

Cottonwood Cove is a Park Service development along the Nevada shoreline of Lake Mohave. It is larger in size than Willow Beach and, unlike Willow Beach, which is in the bottom of Black Canyon, Cottonwood is in the broad Colorado River valley.

I was assigned to the lakeshore cleanup crew. For this job, I would use an old dilapidated, 20-foot johnboat. Typical of the under-funded Park Service, this boat was completely worn out. The paint was worn away and the hull was bent and dented from hundreds of sandy, rocky beachings. Water seeped in around loose rivets and open seams. In fact, the boat would sink if left in the water for more than a day. Each morning, our first order of business was to pump out the almost awash wreck. Once it was floating again we would cast off from the dock and head to our assigned shoreline for a day of walking the beaches and picking up garbage. It is a sad fact that park visitors literally trashed the park as fast as we cleaned it up. Every afternoon we would return to Cottonwood with trash bags mounded so high in the boat that the operator at the stern had to stand to see over the pile.

My family had a boat when I was a kid. We went to the lake often, but Dad was the captain in those days. I really didn't learn to operate a boat until my summer at Cottonwood. Typical of the way things were done back then, on the first day the local maintenance man handed my partner and me the keys to the boat, told us where to find it, and sent us off with only this instruction, "Go to Six Mile Cove. There's lots of trash there." That was as close as it got to training. Consequently, we spent the rest of the summer in the school of hard knocks. We crashed and burned every time we docked.

In June, Eileen came down for a visit. I couldn't take any time off so we could do something special, but we did manage to go camping at Mount Charleston with a mutual college friend over one weekend. What we mostly did was take walks in the semi-cool of the evenings and talk about our plans. I think I did most of the talking. I had plans. I had completely mapped out our—I should really say *my*—future. I would become a ranger, work in a few crown jewel parks and then, after Riffey retired, I would take over his station.

It wasn't out of selfish motives or because of a domineering personality, but I completely failed to factor in Eileen's dreams. As stupid as it sounds, it just did not occur to me that she might have different ideas. While I take full credit for being insensitive, Eileen didn't help by being completely passive when I was going on about my career as a park ranger. All too fast, Eileen's two week stay passed and after she was gone I found myself experiencing something new— loneliness.

In July Mom called to tell me that John Riffey had died, but as a lowly seasonal I felt that I couldn't take time off to attend his funeral. To this day it is one of the few things that I regret. In a rather unusual and magnanimous gesture, the National Park Service allowed John to be buried just down the hill from his home of nearly forty years. On those hot August nights, as I lay in my bed I often thought about Riffey, about my future and what would happen next.

Working at Cottonwood that summer were two student interns, Jane and Lila. They also had grand plans of becoming park rangers one day. But unlike me, these two understood the hiring process and knew what was required to become a seasonal ranger. They told me I needed a certificate from a law enforcement training academy. Up until that time, I had assumed if I worked hard and got a good recommendation, I would be hired. There were just two schools in the country offering this brand new law enforcement training program. The closest school was in Santa Rosa, California. Lila gave me the address and I sent away for an application.

- 4 -

On My Way

My season at Cottonwood ended in September, and in October I reported to the Santa Rosa Criminal Justice Training Center for the intensive 5-week seasonal ranger law enforcement training program. This was the course that all potential rangers had to have before they could be hired. Now that I was finally on the right track, I felt I was on my way to becoming a ranger.

The training center was on the grounds of a former juvenile detention facility and our dorm rooms, which were about four feet wide by ten feet long, had been inmate cells. No meals were provided and because I had little money I survived on cereal and peanut butter sandwiches.

Criminal justice training was all completely new to me. Not satisfied with just our classroom books and handouts, I asked the school's director for more information. He gave me dozens of old or extra books from the school's library. With nothing else to do during the evenings, I spent hours thumbing through the pages.

But I also found time for a practical joke. On the school grounds was an old two-story Victorian mansion. It looked spooky and it was rumored that it was haunted. One day another student and I were poking around the old place and discovered that a back door was unlocked. Realizing the opportunity to substantiate the rumor, we went upstairs and opened one of the dormer windows. The next morning as everyone walked to class we pointed out that the window was open. The next morning the window was closed. The following morning it was open again. Soon everyone believed the ghost stories.

At Santa Rosa I was introduced to the concept of rangers as law enforcement officers. The training included classroom sessions on criminal law, search and seizure, and other relevant subjects. We learned pursuit driving at a nearby race car driving school. We also learned defense tactics, patrol procedures, and proper use of a weapon. At least half of our afternoons were spent on the shooting range learning the finer points of the Smith and Wesson .38 caliber revolver and Remington 870 pump action shotgun.

Because I never saw Riffey with a sidearm, I had never really considered the law enforcement aspect of being a ranger. Even Bill Sherman, my modern example of rangering, didn't act like a cop. Bill had a badge and a gun, yet they seemed to be more like uniform accessories than tools of the trade. At Santa Rosa I learned that indeed rangers were officers of the law. I accepted this reality, but deep down, below the exhilaration of acquiring this new training, I wasn't a law dog.

My real motivation to become a ranger was part reality from a bygone era and part a romantic creation in my mind. The conflict between the concept of rangers as law men and my dream of rangers as helpful public servants would someday meet in painful collision. It would take years, but one day I would have to face the reality that there are no more Tuweep Ranger Stations or Riffeys.

After Santa Rosa I returned home. Eileen was still in school in Reno. Our wedding day was set for June 6th, an appropriate choice because that date is also known as "D day."

Because I couldn't expect my wife to live on peanut butter sandwiches and cereal, I needed to find work. I filed job applications for anything that had some résumé value. The first employment that came along was a security guard at St. Rose De Lima Hospital. I was glad to get it, but the work was agonizingly unchallenging and boring.

During those same fall and early winter months I had continued to apply for better employment. Like always, I applied to the Park Service and was supremely confident that when summer came I would finally get my ranger job. But because I was beginning to feel pressure to have a career going before I became a married man, I also applied to a number of police and fire departments around the state. I didn't really want to be either a policeman or a fireman but, due to the number of disappointments in my quest to become a ranger, I felt I needed a backup plan.

A few weeks later, the Reno Police Department contacted me and scheduled me for employment testing. On the day the MGM hotel in Las Vegas burned, I flew out. After take-off as the plane circled to head north I watched the towering cloud of smoke rise over the MGM hotel and felt a strange sense of sadness. It wasn't about the tragedy developing below. No, the life and death drama only served to remind me that life can be short. I knew deep down I was straying from a dream. What I was about to do was wrong.

Testing for Reno P. D. consisted of a written exam and a physical ability test, followed by an oral board. After successfully completing the written test, the next step was the physical ability test which was held at the track field of a local high school. That's when I saw the competition; hundreds of candidates were sitting in the bleachers waiting their turn on the field. Not knowing what to expect, I hadn't bothered to train. Nevertheless I was in good condition and ended up doing well enough to proceed to the final step.

The next morning I sat before a panel of police officers for my oral board. I hadn't practiced for this either. The board fired questions and, lacking the sophistication to anticipate what they were looking for, all I could do was give honest, straightforward answers. At the end of the inquisition, as I sat miserably on the chair before them, the group held a conference.

Then the chairman spoke and said something to this effect, "We're impressed, we would like to offer you a job, but you know training a police officer is a big investment." He went on, "I think you want to be a ranger. If we hire you and your chance came along to be a ranger, what would you do?" I knew the right answer to this one, if I wanted to get the job. After a pause I replied, "Sir, I'm sorry to have taken up your time. I want to be a ranger." He smiled and said, "If you change your mind, come back."

I moved back to Reno and went to work with the same construction company that I had been with the year before. My old college roommate couldn't take me in but he arranged for me to board with an elderly lady.

As summer drew nearer, I anxiously awaited notification that I was being hired as a ranger. With Santa Rosa behind me, it was all but given. I had three seasons with Lake Mead. I had obtained my CPR card. I had been an auxiliary fireman and a security guard. I had been near the top of my class at the law enforcement academy. I was so confident that I thought I might even get multiple offers. It would be a problem of deciding between Yellowstone and Yosemite.

When it comes to disappointment nothing stings as much as a complete surprise. I got not a single offer. Seasonal ranger applications were numerically scored based in part on the applicant's self evaluation of their skills. Because I had filled out my application honestly, even modestly, my score was too low. It appeared there would be no ranger job this year.

However, Lake Mead once again came through with a maintenance job offer. This season they asked if I would run Willow Beach's maintenance operations. The two permanent employees were gone, one retired and one transferred, and they needed someone to take over. It was an honor to be entrusted with the operation, but my disappointment in not being offered a ranger position tempered my enthusiasm. Nevertheless I accepted the job. I said goodbye to Eileen and headed south once again.

On my first day back in my old stomping ground, District Ranger Bill Sherman greeted me. He expressed how sorry he was that he hadn't been able to hire me, but he said I was just too far down the list. I held my disappointment in, but a little later in the day Bill brought his new seasonal ranger around to meet me. When she stepped out of the patrol vehicle, disappointment stung me again like a fifty-pound bee. The hurt was overwhelming. There was Lila, the volunteer from Cottonwood Cove. She stood there—gun, badge and all. All I could think of was, how could this happen? She had one season as a volunteer. I had three seasons as paid staff. We had been in the same

CPR, Standard First Aid and Santa Rosa classes. How could she get the job when I couldn't? In spite of my pain I smiled, shook hands and wished her well.

Fortunately I had little time for feeling sorry for myself because in little more than a month I would be getting married.

I am guilty as charged, if the charge is being a typical male dog. I did nothing to help Eileen prepare for our wedding. I literally just showed up. Afterwards we spent three days at Lake Tahoe. This mini honeymoon was a gift from my mom and arranged for by Cousin Sharon, who worked at Lake Tahoe.

Then we moved in with my parents. It was never intended to be anything more than a temporary accommodation, but still it was awkward. If that wasn't bad enough, within a week I abandoned Eileen and went out for ten days on a wildland fire. She was left with my parents and nothing to do. I was lucky to still be married when I returned home, but she knew I was a better person than my actions reflected. In spite of that poor start we've had a long and happy marriage.

- 5 -

Shivwits

I was busy sharpening a saw at the work bench in the maintenance shop when Bill Sherman entered. Wasting no time on idle chit-chat, he immediately said he'd been talking about me with the Assistant Chief Ranger Bud. So why would he talk to the Chief about me? Without answering my unspoken question, Bill explained there was a place called Shivwits at the extreme upstream end of Lake Mead where the park abutted Grand Canyon National Park. It was a forested high plateau on the north side of the Grand Canyon. While I had been at Lake Mead for three seasons, I had never heard of this place. I found this fascinating. But what did it have to do with me?

Bill explained that every year, for many years, a retired couple from Temple Bar had been stationed at the Shivwits fire camp from June to September. The agency had just been informed that the husband had become ill so the couple couldn't return. The park desperately needed someone to take their place.

Now I knew what this had to do with me and I could hardly believe my ears. My ranger career had seemed hopelessly derailed, but now by pure luck I was going to be a ranger. Not only a ranger, but a ranger on the Arizona Strip, right next door to Riffey's old stomping ground. This was my chance to walk in Riffey's footsteps. This was my dream come true.

I rushed to Bud's office. It was hard to control my excitement and listen, as I waited for him to explain everything Bill had told me all over again. When he finally got to the job offer I practically shouted, "Yes!" One of the things Bud did say—that I paid no mind to—was that Shivwits Fire Station was remote and very, very primitive. Because of the summers I had spent on the family ranch, to me primitive was just code talk for fun. It never occurred to me that others, like Eileen, might feel differently.

Behind Bud's office was a small room—his cache. In this locked chamber were all the toys of the Ranger Division. There were firearms, duty leather, flashlights, batons, binoculars, goodies of every kind. I'm sure Bud enjoyed my enthusiasm as he led me into his cache. In addition to ranger equipment, Bud had a stock pile of old uniforms given to the park by retiring employees. He picked out a worn felt Smokey the Bear hat and handed it to me. I was thrilled. He went on to pick out a complete uniform and then he topped off the moment by handing me a slightly too large dress service coat. He said, "Someday you're going to need this." Only Chiefs and Superintendents ever wear these formal and expensive jackets. It was a completely useless item for a lowly seasonal manning a remote outpost, but it was a grand gesture.

Over the next few weeks I met my new boss, a ranger stationed at Echo Bay, and together we gathered the things I would need and made plans for the summer. To me the pace of preparations was agonizingly slow. I was ready to go the day they told me I had the job. Finally, the day came. In early July, I headed out with my Jeep pickup loaded to overflowing with radios, pots and pans, food, tools, first aid supplies, spare tires, water, gas, and everything else we would need for a self-sufficient camp at the edge of the civilized world. The trip was about two hundred and thirty miles from doorstep to doorstep and took the greater part of a day to complete.

After stopping in St. George to visit Grandma and top off all fuel tanks, I drove the dusty 92 miles to the Shivwits Fire Station. My mission was to open up the fire camp and get things ready for Eileen and my boss Mike's arrival a few days later. I was hired to work full-time, and Eileen was hired as a part-time firefighter. At least on paper, with my five days a week and her two, the camp was fully manned week in and week out. The reality was that days on or off, hours on or off were meaningless at Shivwits. Home was the ranger station. There was no where else to go. Everyday existence and work blended together into life's routine.

The Shivwits Fire Station was established primarily as a forest fire lookout and also served as a base camp for fire crews should there be a fire in the vicinity. In the 1970s, there had also been a Youth Conservation Corps (YCC) camp next door, but by 1981 little remained of it. Even though the Shivwits Plateau is almost completely covered by forest, wildland fires were not a big problem. Nevertheless the dominant management thinking at the time was that every fire had to be suppressed and done so as aggressively as possible. In just a few years, the thinking would radically change and fire would be viewed as part of the environment, but that summer my job was to put out all fires.

The station was located near the edge of the forest in a grove of ponderosa pines. It looked over a sagebrush and grass covered meadow. Mount Dellenbaugh—a rocky volcanic cone, projecting several hundred feet above the relatively flat plateau—rose up behind the camp. Farther south, forming the southern boundary of my patrol area, was the Grand Canyon. Over thousands of years, wind and water had created deep gashes in the Shivwits Plateau, leaving long peninsulas sticking out into the canyon. Viewed from above, this pattern of erosion resembled the branches of a tree—small gullies became larger gorges that fed into still larger canyons that led into the Grand Canyon.

I arrived at the camp a little before dark. The first thing I saw was the ancient dilapidated 1940s' vintage trailer set up on blocks. This seven-foot wide, twenty-foot long trailer would be our home for the next several months. Its faded, green, metal skin gave way to an interior of dried-out wood paneling, worn-out linoleum, appliances that were older than me, and mouse droppings. Holding my nose, I explored the three tiny rooms: a bedroom, a bathroom—almost too small for one person to stand in and containing only a small sink—and the kitchen/ living room. The kitchen sink had running cold water, a feature that was definitely handy, and a nice two-burner propane stove. The refrigerator was located outside on the porch.

What the trailer didn't have was a toilet. For that business, there was an outhouse at a discreet distance away. Also there was no facility for a bath. Because water had to be hauled in and was more valuable than gold, cleanliness was discouraged. If insisted upon, one could bathe out of a wash pan or go out behind the trailer and stand under the raised water tank and shower. The water tank, on stilts and about ten feet in the air, was fitted with a hose bib and shower head. If you could tough out the icy water and didn't mind exhibiting yourself to all of nature, a shower could be had. Another comfort, lacking but highly desirable, as I would discover when winter approached, was heat. There was no heater, furnace, or fireplace. Thermal comfort was strictly a function of how much clothing one could wear.

The one feature of the ranger station that I really enjoyed during my stay at Shivwits was the deck that ran the length of the trailer. That summer, I spent many an hour sitting on the deck, looking out onto the great sage valley beyond the trees. In the mornings, I would eat my breakfast and plan my day sitting on the edge of the deck. In the evenings, I watched the deer come out of the forest and pass by the camp. Sunsets viewed from the deck were spectacular and when dusk turned to darkness I could witness the magical appearance of thousands of stars.

However, that first day I only gave the deck a nod of approval before exploring the rest of the camp. I soon found the camp had everything needed to live a comfortable Third World lifestyle. There was a little shed behind the trailer that was the "Laundromat," complete with a 1940s' gasoline-powered washing machine with wringer.

Electricity for the station was provided by a 1948 one-cylinder Witte diesel generator, an old relic that sat out in the open about 100 yards from the trailer. This distant placing of the "Shivwits Light and Power Company" was to reduce the effect of the slow, rhythmic thumping. Unfortunately, sounds traveled in the clear mountain air; Eileen and I learned to live with the heartbeat of the old Witte.

Even though this was before the days of cell and satellite phones, we were not completely cut off from the rest of the world. The

Park Service provided us with a two-way radio, but this was strictly for park business.

Because Shivwits was primarily a fire station, there was a fire equipment cache. This was a twenty-foot box trailer set on blocks. It housed helmets, shovels, canteens, sleeping bags, kitchen kits, and great quantities of other stuff intended to outfit a twenty-five-man fire crew. All of this equipment was new, mostly still in boxes, yet years old and most likely destined never to be used.

There was also a walled tent house on the grounds to accommodate crews when they came to fight the big one. With wooden walls about four feet high, a canvas roof, and four metal cots, this was the "Shivwits Hilton." But the most impressive piece of architecture on the grounds was the steel Butler building. It was the camp's garage and workshop. It featured a concrete floor and a stout work bench across the back wall. Everything at Shivwits except this building was junk that had been hauled in from some place else as a make-do until the park could afford better.

After a quick look around, I decided I couldn't stay in the trailer until I cleaned it up. When I had opened the door I had been greeted by a strong, stagnant, and musty odor of rodent nesting. Mouse droppings covered everything—floor, shelves, and countertops. I figured the Butler building would make a good bedroom for my first night. I propped the two wide garage doors open and set up a cot I had found in the center of the room.

In a strange way, even though I had never been here before, I felt like I had come home. This was the culmination of everything that had come before. This was where I belonged. My childhood on the ranch, my dedication in college, my sweaty days in the campgrounds of Willow Beach had all foretold of this my first day as a ranger at my ranger station in the wilds of the Arizona Strip.

Soon after sunset I found myself in a dark, silent world. I had not yet started the old Witte generator so there was neither light nor sound in the camp. The nearest man-made lights were about a hundred miles to the north, and thousands of stars began sparkling in the night sky. Here was beauty I had not known since my days at the ranch.

I wasn't tired yet but in the darkness there was nothing I could do, so I decided to turn in early. I slipped my boots off and without bothering to undress laid down on the cot. The interior of the garage was absolute blackness, but outside I could make out the silhouetted trees against the night sky. At first the silence was broken only now and then by the murmuring moan of the pines as a puff of air passed.

There was a lot to do to get ready for Eileen's arrival and I was going over the things I had to do, when a distinct thump snapped me back to the present. I strained to listen. At first there were no more sounds, then I heard it again. Something was moving, something walking softly somewhere in the garage. I held my breath. My heart was racing. I dared not move. I was not alone. Next I heard the pattering of small feet in the metal rafters above me. Mice! Over the next few minutes I listened to the sounds. At first it seemed to be just one creature moving about. Soon, however, it turned into a full blown parade. There were running feet, rustling paper and canvas, creaking and bumping.

The ranch had prepared me for living and working at a place like Shivwits. I was not afraid to be alone in the wilderness and I was not bothered by "bumps in the night"—that is, normally. Tonight, however, was a different matter. The commotion was more than I could stand. Amplified in the metal garage, the sounds were beginning to stir my imagination. Soon I decided the sounds were too loud to be mice. It must be pack rats, ground squirrels, or even something larger. That last prospect, the unknown was very disconcerting. After a few minutes more, I decided it would be prudent to move my cot outside and leave the garage to the unseen occupants.

I set up my bed in front of the garage and, for extra protection, placed my newly issued .357 Smith and Wesson revolver on the ground beside the cot. I listened to the disturbance in the garage for a while before fading off into sleep.

Suddenly, I was wide awake in full alarm. I was under attack. Something had jumped onto the cot, had landed on my feet. I screamed and rolled to my right, dove for my firearm. I flailed about searching for my weapon, and then I realized the attack was over. The night was quiet except for my rapid breathing. Staring into the pitch black, I listened. I was alone. As my heart rate slowed, reality began to take hold. A mouse had jumped on my bunk. He was probably more scared than I was. But at least I hadn't found my gun and blown my foot off.

All the next day I worked to get the camp opened, cleaned up, and ready for Eileen's arrival. On the third day, I drove the eight miles to Buster Esplin's Wildcat Ranch where a roughly straight and level section of the dirt road doubled as an airstrip. A tattered, orange windsock on a rusty twenty-foot section of pipe flapped in the breeze over the dust and dried cow-pies—"Wildcat International Airport."

At the prearranged time, the park's high-wing Cessna airplane appeared over the western edge of the plateau. After a low pass to inspect the runway, the pilot landed the plane in a cloud of dust. On board were Eileen and my boss Mike. Eileen, still excited about the trip up and our reunion, didn't seem to notice her surroundings at first, but by the time the three of us had made it back to camp, the choking dust, rattling old jeep and jarring bumps had begun to dampen her spirits. My first impression of the camp had been, "Oh boy!" Eileen's first impression was, "Oh my God!" As Mike and I unloaded the jeep, Eileen silently looked around. Now, 30 years later, I can see how traumatic this moment was for my new bride. Here she was committed to spend her life with a man she still did not completely know, a man who thought dust, dirt, an outhouse toilet, and a tiny trailer in the middle of nowhere was romantic. This was not how married life was supposed to be.

Eileen bore her disappointment without comment but I could clearly see her pain. After lunch I suggested that once the well was working, when we could pump some water, things would be better. She could clean up and would feel better.

The three of us drove the one mile to the well. Eileen sat in the truck as Mike and I hooked up the Briggs and Stratton engine to the well's pump. Finally after an hour of fussing and adjusting the motor sputtered to life, driving the big rocking arm of the pump up and down. Like an oil well, the rocking horse creaked and slowly lifted the water. As I waited for the cool, clean water to come surging out of the three-inch hose, I looked over at Eileen in the truck and saw the wet track of a tear that had run down her cheek. The pain I felt at the sight was real. Then swoosh, out came the first stream of water. Just as I was about to call out, "Look, see it will be okay," the next thing that flowed out was a bird's nest, feathers and skeletal remains. I shoved the hose behind my back and glanced over to see if Eileen had seen what happened. She was looking away, looking at something far, far away. I let the hose flush out for a while before I stuck it in the water tank and began filling what would eventually be our washing, cleaning, and drinking water. Mike witnessed the whole incident and prudently never said a word.

An hour later, I drove Mike back to Wildcat for his flight home, back to civilization—back to a world filled with people, telephones, tap water, and store bought things. As I watched the plane fade away, slowly becoming a distant speck, I asked myself, "How could I have been so thoughtless?" Right then, I made a silent promise to Eileen that I would make it up to her. Things would be better and maybe, just maybe, she'd grow to love this place and this life as much as I did.

- 6 -

Fire

The Shivwits Ranger Station existed for only one reason—wildland fire suppression. Not that there were a lot of fires there, but the thinking was that. in an area so remote, if a fire did get started, it could theoretically grow quite large before it would be discovered. Because a fire lookout was needed, the camp was placed at the toe of Mount Dellenbaugh and a road of sorts was bulldozed nearly to its summit. Such a thing could never happen now, but in the early days such projects were commonplace. It was a good choice for a lookout, however, for nearly all of the Shivwits' hundred thousand plus acres could be seen from the conical mountain top.

I became quite aware that Eileen did not share my enthusiasm for our primitive lifestyle. Even though I knew she hated the camp, I thought that, if I showed her the magnificent beauty of the Shivwits Plateau, her feeling would change. So the day after she arrived, I invited her to go with me to the top of Mount Dellenbaugh.

She happily climbed into the jeep and away we went. We followed a faint bulldozed track that was not really a road. It was a little rough, but Eileen was being a good sport until the jeep dropped into a ditch and my tiny wife bounced up hitting her head on the top of the cab. Right then I knew this had not been a good idea.

When we reached the end of the "road" we were still a hundred yards from the summit. We walked to the top and the view was magnificent. To the north, I could see all the way to the Pine Valley Mountains behind St. George. To the west, the sagebrush valley and piñon/juniper covered hills stretched to the westernmost prominence of the plateau—Snap Point. Below Snap, the Grand Canyon ended and Lake Mead began. I turned to the east, where I knew the ranch and Riffey's ranger station were. Of course I couldn't see either of these places. But I did see Mount Trumbull. Beyond the north/south canyons at the edge of the plateau were several mountains, and tallest among them was Mount Trumbull, guardian of the ranch. I pointed out this landmark for Eileen, but where I saw a million memories, she saw only wilderness.

Next I pointed south to the best view of all, the Grand Canyon. Millions of people see the Grand Canyon each year, but only a handful have seen it from the top of Mount Dellenbaugh. Here the canyon is much as it was before the arrival of the Europeans. It is raw, untamed, and unspoiled. In contrast to Grand Canyon's North and South rims, there are no lodges, campgrounds, concessions, or very few roads. Best of all, to my way of thinking, there were no people on Shivwits except for a couple of ranchers and two very green fire guards.

During the trip back to camp, Eileen had nothing to say. I reined in my enthusiasm and concentrated on the road as I eased the Jeep over the boulders and tried to keep from bouncing my bride off the seat.

During the next couple of weeks, Eileen and I settled in and established a routine. The camp was a mess and we spent many hours squaring things away. To give a little more civilized feel to the place, I erected a TV antenna on top of the water tank which gave us one snowy channel out of Las Vegas. It was more like watching radio than television but Eileen appreciated the gesture. Mice were a continuing problem, so in the evenings Eileen would sit in her chair with her legs drawn up, listen to TV, and watch the mice scurry across the floor.

Shivwits was a fire lookout camp and our reason for being there was to watch for forest fires. Human-caused fires were not an issue. Mother Nature was the fire bug. If there was a fire, it would be started by lightning. Consequently the only time it was necessary to man the lookout—Mount Dellenbaugh—was after thunderstorms.

July started out hot and dry, but by mid-month the monsoon began. Each afternoon, cumulus clouds appeared on the horizon. These clouds thickened and grew and, by late afternoon, distant rumbling thunder announced the presence of dark, ominous thunderheads, but we got little or no rain, just promises.

Like a duty-bound servant, each day after the storms and again first thing the next morning, I walked the two miles to the summit of Dellenbaugh to scout for fires. Our one trip up the mountain in the jeep had been enough to convince me that walking was not only more pleasant but faster too. On the mountain top, I would spend several hours looking about and, as boredom set in, I daydreamed. I could see myself at Toroweap. Riffey's station would one day be mine.

One day I decided to look for the inscription, "W Dunn 1869" which I had been told was near the summit of Mount Dellenbaugh. This signature is supposedly evidence that William Dunn, a member of Major John Wesley Powell's party on an exploratory descent of the Colorado River in 1869, made it to Mount Dellenbaugh before he and his two companions disappeared. I had read about Major Powell's exploration of the Grand Canyon and I knew the story of Separation Canyon south of the Shivwits Plateau where three members of Powell's group had left the river to climb the canyon walls and walk to the nearest Mormon settlement, St. George.

The inscription is small and hard to find. I didn't locate it the first time I looked, but after several explorations of the area I spotted the tiny letters scratched onto a lava rock on a ridge southeast of the summit. One wonders at the location of this signature. Why isn't it at the top of the mountain as a record of Dunn's having achieved the highest point? I also noted that a few others have signed and dated the nearby rocks. Perhaps homesteaders and cowboys seeing the inscription and attaching no historical significance to the name and date have concluded that this is a place to register—the place to make known that you too have stood on the summit of Mount Dellenbaugh.

Before leaving Dunn's name and date, I stood and carefully considered the view. More that 100 years later I was seeing the same plateaus and canyons that he had seen and I'm certain the view was the same, but with my fully provisioned camp only two miles away I'm also certain that my feelings were not the same.

41

Every day I stood atop Mount Dellenbaugh and searched the surroundings for smoke, but saw none. I anxiously waited for a fire. Then one afternoon a noisy thunderstorm passed directly over the camp. It spit only a few drops of rain but the booming threats from the sky were impressive and I knew some of the strikes were close to camp. After supper about 6:30 that evening I walked out onto the deck, looked across the valley and spotted a small column of blue smoke. Since the sun sets around 8:30 in July on the Shivwits, I knew if we set out immediately we could reach the fire before dark. This was it. This was what we were here for, yet for one full minute I stood paralyzed. What should I do? My paralysis was understandable. I had received no training for this event, even though Eileen and I had been hired as fire technicians and sent to Shivwits to fight fires.

As suddenly as it had grasped me the panic passed and excitement took its place. There, straight in front of me, across the valley coming up from behind a dark timber covered ridge was a fire. It looked close, no more than two miles away.

I called out to Eileen that we had a fire and set off for the Butler building to get the tools—shovels and Pulaski axes that we were going to need. After quickly loading the jeep I spread a topographic map of the area across the kitchen table. With Eileen looking on I plotted where I thought the fire was. It was clear we would have to walk at least a mile from the nearest road.

Ready, we headed out. We bounced our way down some ancient tracks that barely passed as a road. When we had gone as far as we could by jeep, we began hiking. Navigating through the forest was more difficult than I had anticipated. The terrain was mostly flat and there were no landmarks for orientation. The piñon and juniper trees grew close together making it impossible walk in a straight line. We were continuously forced off our course to go around the scrubby trees. I was concerned because if we didn't find the fire before dark we might not find it until the next day.

After half an hour we stopped and I climbed a juniper. From the treetop I saw the smoke rising out of the forest a few hundred yards away.

When we arrived we found a small, half-acre ground fire, creeping slowly through the needle duff under a stand of ponderosa pines. The fire was in a draw and while there were few flames, the smoke was thick in the still air. After a quick look around I outlined my plan. I knew from tagging along with my grandfather, who had been a fire warden for the U.S. Forest Service, that we should build a fire line around the fire.

A line scratched to mineral soil would separate the fire from its fuel supply. I said I would go first, clearing the line with a shovel and instructed Eileen to follow chopping out any roots I missed with the Pulaski. It was hot, smoky work. The sun had gone down just as we arrived and now the smoke hung low in the forest creating a horror movie fog effect. Each of us wore a headlamp which illuminated small circles of ground at our feet. As I worked I could hear behind me the steady thumping of Eileen's Pulaski seeking out roots. She was almost invisible, enveloped in darkness and smoke just a few feet behind me. Yet when I would catch a glimpse she was always bent over, head down, concentrating on her task and working the tool with all the strength of her small body. This girl I had married was a real trouper and I was proud of her.

After a couple of hours the line was complete and we had even mopped up much of the smoldering fire. We sat down on a log to rest. During the work we hadn't spoken much and just as I was about to say something, Eileen said, "This isn't a very good tool, it doesn't cut." I looked at the Pulaski. I couldn't believe it—the metal sheaths that covered and protected the sharp blades were still tightly fastened in place. She had been working with covers over the blades. Looking at the Pulaski then at Eileen's tired and ash smeared face, I knew this was definitely not the time to laugh.

Eileen's next comment, which now seems even funnier was, "Which way to the jeep?" In the dark and after circling the fire several times I now suddenly realized that I had no idea which direction to go to get back to our jeep. After a long pause I admitted that I didn't know.

Eileen is almost impossible to rattle. Lost in the forest, a hundred miles from anyone, in the middle of the night—no problem. In the void of my leadership she confidently announced, "This is the way." I looked in the direction she pointed and said, "No, it's this way," and pointed in a different direction. Eileen wasn't convinced, but I asserted my authority. I said she was wrong and I was right. Before the night was over I regretted not listening to her.

With my leading the way we started for home, but nothing looked familiar. In a few minutes I realized I was lost. Not simply lost, but completely disoriented. I had no idea which way was north, let alone which way to the jeep. We could just as easily be walking away from the jeep as toward it. I didn't want to admit defeat, but how long should I let male machismo keep me from letting Eileen know I was lost?

Finally I called a halt to our march. As we stood there in the darkness I heard a faint deep chug, chug. The sound of the camp's Witte generator drifted softly in the night air. With it as a homing beacon we gave up trying to find the jeep and began the long hike back to camp.

Around mid-August my parents came for a visit. While my mom had grown up on the Strip, she had never been over to the Shivwits area, so they were curious. Their unexpected visit provided a fortuitous opportunity. Eileen had tried hard to adjust to life at camp, but it just wasn't in her. She was unhappy. Furthermore, she still had a year of college before graduation. We talked it over and we both agreed that it made sense for her to resign, go home with my parents, and return to school. When the fire season was over in September I would rejoin her in Reno. It was a bittersweet parting. I was sad to see her go, but I knew it was the right and smart thing to do. Finishing college was a very important first step to a brighter future.

However, I wouldn't be alone. The family dog, Dingo, was left with me. Dingo was a wire-haired mutt and for the remainder of my time at Shivwits we would be a team.

- 7 -

In Riffey's Footsteps

With Eileen gone, the routine at Shivwits changed considerably. I no longer had any particular reason to hang around the camp, so with lots of time on my hands, I became far more adventurous. In fact, I began to operate the way I figured Riffey would have operated. I dropped the official ranger or firefighter uniform in lieu of T-shirts and blue jeans. My work hours became irregular. I started my day whenever I got around in the morning and finished the day whenever the work was done. While that sounds like laziness, in reality I worked longer and harder than I had before. I averaged ten to twelve hours a day, seven days a week.

First I decided to fix up the camp. The place, for all its charm, was really a dump and a disgrace as a government facility. I thinned out the small trees in a nearby stand of ponderosa pines and used the logs to rebuild the fence around the camp. Next I policed up all of the trash, junk, and other useless refuse that had been left at the camp over the years and had a huge bonfire. I cleaned and organized the fire cache and the Butler building. After that I built a shed around the Witte and made a loading dock for the 50-gallon drums of diesel that fueled the old generator. I rebuilt the tent bunkhouse that had all but collapsed and added a hard roof, screened it in, and gave it a fresh coat of paint.

But my biggest improvement to the camp was the construction of a 10 x 10-foot office at one end of the trailer's wooden deck. With Mike's permission, I purchased a truckload of lumber in St. George and in a matter of a few days I had a very respectable office. I moved the big, noisy radio out of the trailer and set it up in the new station.

Complete with maps on the walls, a roughly built desk and some deer antlers over the door, the place looked very rangerly. The funny thing about the whole deal was that after all that effort, I spent very little time in my office. My life was lived in the field.

It had only taken a few weeks to transform the camp into a smart-looking ranger outpost, complete with a twenty-foot flag pole. I had worked sun up to sun down every day because this was *my* ranger station.

The closest thing I had to a day off was when about every three weeks I would drive in to St. George for supplies, groceries, and mail. Consequently, going to town was a big event. As groceries began to dwindle, I would begin planning my trip. I would make a list of things needed and load drums for gasoline and diesel into the jeep truck. Whenever possible I tried to make my trip on days when it was going to rain. Because I felt that I was walking in my grandpa and Riffey's footsteps, I actively sought the kind of challenges and adventures they had had. My grandfather had taught me that getting stuck in the mud was just a fact of life on the Arizona Strip and nothing to fear. He also taught me how to get unstuck or, if that failed, how to be patient and wait until the road dried out. For that possibility I always carried food, water, and a sleeping bag for a roadside campout.

Grandma lived in St. George and when I arrived on her doorstep she treated me like a returning war veteran. We would have a big lunch. Then I would read my mail, saving the letters from Eileen for last. Then came "official business" in the government's truck. My boss told me that banking and buying groceries were considered "official business" as long as I also did something official like picking up a drum of diesel.

While fixing up the camp occupied most of my time, the fire season was still my primary reason for being there. After our first fire I realized I didn't know what I was doing. A bookshelf in the house trailer held some old fire fighting manuals and I began studying these. One day I came across a memorandum in a stack of dusty paperwork which indicated all firefighters had to have a certificate called a "Red Card." I did not have one of these, so I wrote a letter to Bud asking about this. A couple of weeks later the park airplane flew over the camp and dropped my "official mail"—a freshly issued "Red Card," indicating I had done very well on the fitness test and was now a qualified firefighter.

Not long after Eileen left I had my second fire. A late evening thunderstorm pounded the plateau and first thing next morning I hiked to the summit of Dellenbaugh to look for fires. I didn't see any smoke but I lingered there thinking that as the day warmed, if there was a fire it would start smoking. I sat on a rock, elbows to knees, and gazed out over the labyrinth of hazy canyons to the south enjoying the view. Finally I stood up ready to leave, made one last scan and to my surprise saw a small smoke rising out of the forest four or five miles away. In the weeks since Eileen's and my first experience with wilderness fire I had become a little more sophisticated. But as I soon discovered, I still had a lot to learn about both fire fighting and navigation.

Knowing that a road ran north/south about half way between the fire and me, I decided if I drove down the road until my compass bearing's back sight on the summit of Dellenbaugh matched my bearing from the summit to the fire, I could easily walk the remaining distance to the fire by following the compass headings.

I returned to camp, loaded my fire gear in the jeep and drove to the spot indicated by the compass. From the mountain top the fire had looked to be burning in a ponderosa snag. So in addition to the shovel and Pulaski, I took along the antique and very heavy chainsaw that I had found buried under junk in the Butler building. Loaded like a pack mule with compass in hand, I lined up my bearing and started off.

It is impossible to walk in a straight line through a piñon and juniper forest. The scruffy limbs hanging low are forever blocking your way. However, I held my compass in front of me always being careful after each detour to keep the direction arrow lined up. I had traveled no more than a couple hundred yards, when, because I was watching my compass instead of my feet, I tripped and went sprawling across the ground. With nothing hurt but my pride, I gathered up my burden and picked up my compass. But it appeared to be broken. The needle seemed to point in the wrong direction.

I decided it had been damaged when it hit the ground. It never occurred to me that I could be wrong and the compass could be right. I shoved the useless device into my shirt pocket and considered the problem of staying on course. At this point my actions became more reminiscent of a Keystone Cop, than a wilderness firefighter.

I figured if I drifted off line I could walk within ten yards of the fire and never see it. Then I noticed that the shadows of the trees around me all formed the same angle to my proposed line of travel. I seized upon the idea that as long I kept the angle of the shadows the same, I would be going in a straight line. Of course this plan had a couple of serious flaws. First I wasn't on line at the beginning and second as the sun moved across the sky the trees' shadows moved as well.

Off I went. I walked for an hour in a direction that was off course at the start and became further off course with the passage of time. After an hour I was certain the fire had to be close. I climbed a tree and looked about. Nothing. I started out again, stopping often to sniff for smoke and climb trees. Still no sign of fire. Maybe, I thought, the fire had gone out.

Tired and frustrated I trudged on lugging the beastly chainsaw, determined to find the fire. After only a few yards I popped out of the forest onto a road. I was completely puzzled. My map had not shown any roads in this area. Even more surprising was that there were fresh tire tracks going down the road. The mystery deepened for I knew there had been no visitors in weeks to Shivwits. As I stood there considering all this, I heard a vehicle approaching. Shortly thereafter a local rancher, Buster, came around the bend in his old pickup truck. He stopped, pushed his sweat-stained cowboy hat up and greeted me with, "Hiya Chuck! Saw the jeep up the road a ways."

Immediately I knew I had walked in a circle. I was back at the road I had started from. Unwilling to admit I had been lost, I told Buster I was getting ready to head out to a fire. I've wondered in the years since, if my sweaty appearance and red face betrayed me, but that day he asked no questions and I volunteered no information.

The day was half over and I still had a fire to find and fight. I hiked back to the jeep, stripped my gear down to the bare essentials and started out once more. This time my fatigue encouraged common sense. I would pick out a tree, walk to it, pick out another and continue on. Amazingly, I arrived at a 50-foot tall, smoking ponderosa in less than forty-five minutes. I surveyed the problem. Lightning had hit a naked old tree. The track of the energy was plainly evident all the way down one side. Thirty feet up in a crotch between the trunk and a twisted limb was a smoldering fire. No flames could be seen, but smoke steadily puffed up.

There was no climbing this tree. The first limbs on the 3-foot diameter bole were twenty feet above me. I couldn't get up to the fire therefore it would have to come down to me. I would have to fell the old giant. The idea to ignore the fire even occurred to me, but with every puff of breeze a shower of embers would rain down onto the duff below. Clearly, sooner or later, one of those embers would take hold and what was one tree could become a forest fire.

I had never cut down a tree in my life, but I had lugged the chainsaw along. Of course a person had better know what they are doing before attempting to cut down a large tree. In fact, every year firefighters are hurt, even killed, by falling trees. I've heard it said that the Lord looks out for babies and fools. I wasn't a baby. But fortunately, try as I might, the chainsaw wouldn't start. Finally giving up, I looked to my Pulaski. With the first swing of the axe I knew this plan was doomed. The trunk was like tempered steel. With each blow the Pulaski stung my hands, but dislodged only a few small chips. After ten minutes of this work I had produced scarcely a dent in the tree's bark.

Then I noticed the soil was cool and damp. Maybe I could smother the fire with mud balls. The idea sounds crazy, because it was crazy. But with the enthusiasm and determination of a greenhorn I started throwing mud balls at the smoking notch. It was a small target and the trajectory was lousy. I hurled mud ball after mud ball scoring less than one in twenty hits. After an hour mud clung all over the tree, my arm ached and blue smoke still puffed up from the notch. Exhausted and frustrated I lay back against a nearby tree and closed my eyes. Just as I was about to drop off to sleep a big drop of water hit me.

From the heavens came my relief. What I hadn't been able to do in ten hours was accomplished in ten minutes. In a soaking rain I carried my useless tools home.

In spite of my questionable performance on the first two fires, I still fancied myself as the quintessential wilderness ranger. I was John Riffey Junior. In my view a ranger was supposed to know everything that there was to know about the land under his charge. Therefore, I made it my new mission to explore the plateau. I began patrolling further and further out. I explored roads, tracks really, that hadn't seen a vehicle in years. I walked old fences and investigated winding canyons. It was exciting. Every time I found something like a long ago forgotten homesteader's cabin or a seep in a canyon wall; I felt I had discovered treasure. When life is good it can be very good and it was good on the Shivwits.

With the oncoming of fall I felt restless. Several of my longer patrols had taken me all the way to the easternmost boundary of the park. I had been in Whitmore Canyon, where Lake Mead National Recreation Area meets with Grand Canyon National Park. On the east side of Whitmore the land rose up into mountains. Just beyond these mountains was Mount Trumbull, the ranch, and Tuweep Ranger Station. Standing in the deep valley of Whitmore and looking up, I felt the longing pull of my past. A silent voice in the breeze and the smell of the sage called to me, "This way, just a little further."

A few days later as I sat on the edge of the porch eating breakfast with Dingo at my side, I started to explain the day's plan. Dingo pretended to listen, but he was really hoping for a scrap of bacon. I often held conversations with Dingo. This morning I stopped in mid-sentence. "No Dingo," I said, "I've changed my mind. Today we're going to visit Riffey."

I knew such a trip was technically an unauthorized lark that would take me fifty miles out of my jurisdiction, but I figured the odds of being caught were slim and, even if I was, I could claim I was making a liaison trip to my neighboring ranger station.

Joyfully, Dingo and I set out. Dingo liked to ride with his head out the window with the cool morning air blowing in his face. And while

I didn't stick my head out, I did roll down the window and enjoyed the familiar smells of sage, pine and dust. The truck rattled and bounced along. With every mile I felt my childhood past returning. My first stop was the old ranch house. Grandpa and Grandma had finally been forced off the land, but it wasn't from the elements. No, only Grandpa's health had been able to drive him back to civilization. Grandpa was gone and the ranch house of my youth was now just another empty shell on the Arizona Strip. However, the ghosts were still there. I walked past the tree house, which my brother and I had remodeled a dozen times; past the cool dugout bedroom where Grandma had read to us on hot summer afternoons; and into the empty house still filled with memories.

After eating our sack lunch on the front porch Dingo and I loaded up and began the last leg of our pilgrimage. I wondered what I would find in Tuweep. John Riffey was also now gone. His passing was the end of an era. This would be my first visit to his grave.

I pulled up to the garage and stopped. The sandstone walls and heavy wooden doors were just as I remembered them. Everything was closed up. There was no sign of any occupants about. I walked up the steep driveway to the house and knocked on the kitchen door. No answer. Walking around to the windows where Riffey's dining room table sat, I peaked in. The room was empty. No one lived here anymore. The Tuweep Station was unmanned.

After Riffey's death, the station either stood empty or was manned part-time by seasonals for several years. The work of rangering was changing and so were the type of people becoming rangers. It was difficult to find people who were willing to live and work in isolated outposts any more.

After poking about for a time, I walked down the road to Riffey's grave. It was a simple plot, just as he would have wanted. I stood there thinking how interesting it was that things in my life tended to go in circles. Riffey had influenced my career even before I knew what I wanted to do and now I was here working and doing just what he did. If only then I had known how many more times my travels would take me back to the beginning. Maybe our destinies are written in the stars.

It was a quiet and reflective trip back to Shivwits. I didn't talk to Dingo and he didn't say anything either. Maybe like me, he was remembering Grandpa and Riffey and the way things used to be.

- 8 -

Goodbye Shivwits

When the fire season was done, I was done; at least that was what Bud told me when he hired me. So I had figured sometime around the end of September I would get my walking papers. But since I was technically a seasonal ranger, not just a firefighter, Bud asked if I would stay on for a few more months and work the deer hunting season. Because I knew this was probably my last opportunity to live my dream, I said yes.

In mid-October Mom and Dad came out for a visit. It was once more fortuitous timing, for my jeep truck quit me the weekend they arrived. The jeep had been an adventure in itself. It was worn out when I got it and between the rough roads and my less than conservative driving, it had a tough summer. Early on I broke a leaf spring. The park mechanic flew out with the parts and together we changed the spring on the runway of the Wildcat Ranch airstrip. Later, on a trip to St. George, the front bumper fell off and I ran over it, poking a hole in the gas tank. Unable to stop the leak I raced the last fifteen miles to town and coasted into the garage as the jeep ran out of fuel.

But the weekend Mom and Dad arrived I didn't know what the problem was. The old jeep just wouldn't start. Dad and I worked on it for hours. We determined that even though the fuel pump appeared to be working and the fuel lines and filter were clean, no fuel was reaching the carburetor. My dad, a master of "where there's a will there's a way," decided if fuel wouldn't flow from the fuel tank to the carburetor then he would bypass the problem. A quick search of the workshop produced the needed innovation—a 1-gallon paint thinner can. He wired the can in place under the hood and re-routed the gas line to it. With the help of gravity, fuel flowed once more and the truck would start. It was a slow process, but at nine miles to the gallon, I limped into St. George. To be truly successful in a place like Shivwits, such resourcefulness was required. Unfortunately, in today's world, such traits have all but disappeared.

November was deer hunting season on the Arizona Strip. Not being a hunter I spent some time with the local State Game Warden to learn the ropes. By opening day of the season I was ready. I didn't know what to expect, but because hunting is popular in Southern Utah, I figured there would be quite a few hunters. I was ready, but only one hunter showed up. He was a bow hunter. The Shivwits Plateau was too far off the beaten track. No sunshine patriots or summer soldiers came this far out.

My bow hunter, from Southern Arizona, stopped at the station on his way out to Kelly Point, a 20-mile-long promontory. This headland protrudes into the Grand Canyon and forces the Colorado River to take a long detour around its southern end on its travel to the sea. Most of Kelly Point is reasonably flat but unbelievably rocky. For long stretches the road that runs down Kelly's spine is nothing more than a pavement of boulders. Consequently the 20-mile, bone-jarring trip to the end of the point took almost five hours. A man could walk almost as fast as he could drive this distance.

After three days, when the bow hunter hadn't returned, I decided I had better check on his welfare. As I drove out to find the hunter I met him on his way back. We stopped, got out, and exchanged greetings. His hunt had been unproductive, but then he mentioned that he had seen bear tracks at Kelly Tank, a small pond near the end of the point. Laughing, I stated that there were no bear in this part of the country. No, he insisted he knew what bear tracks looked like and this was clearly a bear. Well, I didn't believe it, but his insistence was so strong that I decided it was worth the rough trip out to see for myself.

After several hours of bumping along I arrived at Kelly Tank. Not paying much attention to our surroundings, Dingo and I walked out onto the levee and studied the small mud hole. There were only a few inches of water in the bottom surrounded by a wide mud band. Deer and other game tracks crisscrossed the soft ground. Scanning the scene I saw the hunter's footprints. He had walked right up to the edge of the mud and turned around. I followed his prints, and sure enough, they took me to strange new tracks. They looked like bear tracks. I photographed the prints and studied them closely. When I got back to the station I intended to look them up in a wildlife field guide. As I examined the scene I could read the action. First the bear or whatever it was had come down to the water's edge to drink. Then the hunter had followed the tracks down, but wait, then the creature had returned. A second set of tracks were on top of the hunter's. I snapped up straight and scanned the brush all around me. "Dingo, come here," I called. It wasn't for my protection that I called my dog, but out of fear that Dingo might become a bear snack. Together we returned to the jeep. I had never lived in bear country and I had no experience in such matters, but it seemed to me the most prudent thing to do was leave this bear or whatever it was alone. If Kelly Tank was his home I could respect that. Back at the house trailer I looked up the tracks in my wildlife field guide and decided that I had indeed seen bear tracks.

After dinner I settled in for some reading before bedtime. I was tired, for it had been another long day but, like all the rest, a good one. An hour later, feeling sleepy, I turned to Dingo and said, "It's time for bed." He knew the drill and headed for the door. I picked up my flashlight. You see, going to bed at Shivwits wasn't just a matter of climbing into bed. First I had to shut down the power plant, because to run the camp's generator twenty-four hours a day made no sense. I only need power in the morning when I radioed in my morning report and in the evening when I needed lights. The rest of the time the noisy, diesel drinking, dirty machine was turned off.

Paradoxically, there was no electric light in the generator shed. I had to use my flashlight to see the shut-off switch for the throbbing machine. I flipped the switch, the roar of the engine died away and the camp went dark. Outside, hundreds of stars twinkled in the clear night sky and I could see the broad ribbon of the Milky Way. It is a sad fact that most Americans will never see such night skies, let alone live in the wilderness and get to experience simple joys like seeing bear tracks on a pond dam.

With bear tracks still on my mind I turned back toward the trailer. The beam of my flashlight raked across the yard and there at the edge of the black tree line were two red *bear* eyes. They were lit for only an instant by the beam of my flashlight, but with the speed of a super computer my mind analyzed what I had seen and fired off the message to my feet, "It's a bear! Run!" I was fast but Dingo was faster. As I raced toward the trailer Dingo passed me.

Safe in the trailer I suddenly realized I hadn't seen a bear; I had seen Dingo's eyes. In hindsight, I cannot say if I could outrun a bear, but I know I can't outrun a red-eyed mutt.

By the end of November it was cold on the Shivwits. The trailer had no heater so Dingo and I would burrow under a mountain of blankets each night and stay there until the first rays of sun came over the treetops in the morning. When it became light I would peek out and test the air to see if I could see my breath. If I could, I snuggled back down and waited for more sunshine. By mid-morning the days were warm enough to go without a jacket but as soon as the sun set it turned cold again.

As the days were becoming shorter, my project list grew shorter. With little work to do I found myself with an excess of leisure time. Dingo and I would take long walks in the afternoons. On one such walk I returned to the scene of Eileen's and my first fire. I sat on the same log that we had sat on together that night. For the first time it struck me how much I missed her. With my knife I scratched her name on an adjacent boulder. Technically it was not the thing to do, but it was understandable at the moment.

My final instructions from my boss were to close the camp for the season when "the first snow flies." I didn't want the season to end, for in my heart I knew I would never live this kind of life again, yet I was anxious to be with Eileen once more. Finally the day came when Dingo and I awoke to a slate gray sky and a skiff of snow covering the ground. It was time to go. With little enthusiasm I began winterizing the camp and packing up. The next morning the adventure came to an end. I drove out the gate, stopped, got out to close it behind me for the last time and stood there looking at the pitiful camp. It still wasn't much to look at, but it had been my ranger station. It had been home and it had been all that I could have asked for.

Looking back, after all of these years, after all the adventures that followed, after successes and promotions and after new places and jobs, Shivwits and that old fire camp are still the highlight of my career. For never have I been more alive, more happy, more in my element than I was during those simple days of summer and fall of 1981. As I drove away then, I doubted if I would ever return.

- 9 -

Detour

Back again with Eileen in Reno, I found myself unemployed, bored, and at a loss as to what to do next. After seeing Eileen's unhappiness at Shivwits, I knew she would never share my dream of one day taking over Riffey's Tuweep Ranger Station. Even though I still wanted to be a ranger, I had to consider Eileen's needs and wishes.

As hard as it was to think about it, I knew I had to consider other options. If I was going to be forced into something else it would have to meet certain basic requirements. I needed freedom. My career should be an outdoor job if at all possible. It definitely could not be an office or desk job. It also had to be exciting. Accountant, banker, and assembly line worker were clearly out. When my brother Dave's friend told me he planned to join the Air Force after college, I realized that fit my criteria. The more I thought about it, military combat pilot seemed like a good possibility. When I mentioned the idea to Eileen she had no reservations.

A few days later I walked to the United States Air Force recruiter's office and proudly stated I wanted to be a pilot. I listened to the recruiter describe my future with the Air Force and signed up. Actually, before I could be accepted I had to pass an intensive physical and rather difficult officer's candidate school and flight aptitude tests. The tests would come first and I only had a couple of months to prepare for the next scheduled exam.

I've been called a lot of things, but scholarly was never one of them. Knowing my limitations, I bought every study and test guide I could find. Since Eileen was going to school during the day and working at a department store in the evenings and I was unemployed I had nothing better to do than study. I spent hours and hours working problems and reading test prep books.

While being a pilot in the Air Force wasn't my first career choice, nor did it hold for me the same sense of life's purpose as being a ranger; it was my new direction. This was a huge opportunity and I felt I couldn't afford to fail. Consequently, on the eve of my exam I did something I had never done before, I slipped away from the apartment, went to the nearby Catholic church and prayed.

The Air Force bused me to McClellan AFB in Sacramento, California, for the test, which was six hours of intense and timed hell. At the end of the day I was exhausted. The only thing I knew for sure was that I had blown it. So many of the problems had, after my best effort, come down to a guess. Two weeks later the recruiter telephoned. Because I was certain he would tell me that I had set a new record for the all time lowest score, I ignored his message. After several days of refusing to return his phone calls I finally worked up the courage to receive the bad news.

Surprisingly, when I mustered the courage to call, the recruiter said, "Congratulations son, you did an outstanding job!" Then he explained that I had scored high on the aptitude portion of the test for navigator and well enough to be considered for pilot. Now the Air Force must have needed navigators that day because he gave me a long speech about a guaranteed position if I would take navigator. There was no guarantee if I chose pilot, and I would have to pass an oral board. I couldn't afford to take a chance. So I chose navigator.

The next step was a flight physical. If I passed that I would be in. The physical, while very thorough, was not particularly remarkable except for one small point. During the exam the physician pointed to a small dark mole on my chest and said, "What's that?" I had never noticed the spot before. I said I didn't know what it was and he suggested that I should have it checked out. I wondered what the big deal was about a mole and because I didn't have the money for unnecessary doctor's visits, I ignored his suggestion.

With all of the testing completed, I was accepted and given my class date and orders. I would be attending Officer Training School in December, still many months away. In the meantime I needed a job.

Things were looking pretty desperate until the Nevada Division of State Parks called. When I had returned to Reno after my season at Shivwits I had applied for a position with State Parks, and they were just now offering me a seasonal ranger job at Lake Lahonton State Recreation Area. I needed money while I waited for Officer Training School, so I took the job.

Finally, the day arrived when I was to leave for Officer Training School. Eileen and her dad saw me off at the Greyhound Bus Station. Before I boarded the bus they gave me a relatively expensive Saco "aviator" looking wristwatch. It was at that moment as I accepted the watch and said goodbye to Eileen that I realized the seriousness of my decision to join the Air Force. This wasn't simply something interesting to do. This was no game. Eileen and her dad were counting on me.

From Reno I traveled to Oakland, California, to the induction center and then on to San Antonio, Texas, and Lackland A.F.B., where I would attend Officer Training School for twelve weeks. In Oakland I was joined by a dozen other inductees. We were sworn in by a gruff talking, scary looking Marine captain. As I raised my hand I knew there was no turning back.

My first day in the military was a long one. Our flight didn't arrive in San Antonio until midnight. From the airport we were bused to the base. It was the longest bus ride of my life. With each mile I grew more and more tense. I had no idea what to expect, but I was sure whatever was about to happen wasn't going to be pleasant. As we passed through the base's gate I braced for abuse. The bus lurched to a stop in front of an old two-story barracks. Sweating with fear I quickly piled off the bus with the other inductees and we formed two very unmilitary like lines.

An upper classman greeted us with "Good evening, gentlemen. Welcome to OTS." He pointed, "Go in that building over there. Draw sheets, blankets, and a pillow. Go upstairs, find yourself a bunk and I'll see you in the morning. That's all." I couldn't believe what I had heard. No insults. No yelling. No pushups. This was my kind of Air Force.

BAAA!.... I was awakened by an overwhelming noise. I went from dead asleep to wide-eyed terror. Without pause I sat straight up and leaped from the top bunk. Now I must point out that OTS has got to be one of the cleanest places on earth. Hospital operating room custodians could take lessons from Officer Candidates on cleanliness. The floors are buffed to a mirror like gloss. When my socked feet hit that slick surface they didn't even slow down. Bam! I landed flat on my back. The blow knocked the air out of me. Gasping, I looked straight up into the face of a mean-looking officer. He was shouting something. At first I couldn't understand, but as my senses returned, his words came to me loud and clear. "Are you sleeping on my floor OT? On your feet, now."

"Yes sir," I sputtered.

All basic training shares common denominators: inspections, marches, classes and drills. OTS was no different, and very quickly, routines develop. I was beginning to adjust to my new world when something happened that turned everything upside down. A couple of weeks into our training all flight personnel were given another comprehensive physical. As I stood before the flight surgeon, clad only in my shorts, he scanned my records and then gave the classic warning signal, "Hmmm." He picked up a ruler and placed it on my chest. Then he said, "Hmmm," once more, followed by, "OT, I'm sending you over to see a specialist."

On the bus ride over to the main base hospital I tried to figure out what all the fuss was about. Surely a mole was nothing serious. I felt fine. When I arrived at the dermatology department I was seen by a kindly, middle-aged man. He introduced himself as a dermatologist and surgeon. He immediately examined the "mole" on my chest.

After a time he sat down on a stool and said something to this effect, "I think it's melanoma, which is a type of skin cancer." But before I could react, he continued, "You'll be okay. We're going to get it in time." The man was so fatherly and calm that I felt no apprehension.

Within half an hour I was on the operating table. I was given local anesthesia and chit-chatted with the doctor and nurses while the offending mole was cut away. Later while being bandaged the doctor stated it was a little bigger than expected, but he still believed there would be no problems. They would examine the tissue in the lab to make sure they had got it all. The doctor told me that he would call me in three or four days with the results.

I left the hospital upbeat and cheerful. In a strange twist of logic I couldn't believe how unbelievably lucky I was. My inability to get hired as a ranger had led me to seek an alternative. Had I not entered the Air Force I would not have discovered the cancer until it was too late. The path I had chosen, or maybe was directed down, had been life saving. I was literally living Robert Frost's poem, "The Road Not Taken."

I was required to check back in with the flight surgeon before I returned to my unit. In the flight surgeon's office I handed him the records that I had hand carried from the dermatologist. "Hmmm," he said and then the speech started. I don't remember exactly how it went but it was close to, "OT, do you know what melanoma is?" Without pause, the performance continued. "Are your things in order? Do you have a will?" What! This wasn't the take the specialist had outlined. He'd said everything was okay. But the flight surgeon's words were a contradiction of the dermatologist's message. At first I was stunned and then slowly I began to understand. Things were not good, but very, very bad. I was going to die. I don't know what else the flight surgeon may have said for I heard nothing more. My mind was already racing ahead and trying to reconcile the two very different prognoses. The only answer that made sense was that the flight surgeon was being brutally honest and the dermatologist was trying to shield me from my harsh and short future. I left the flight surgeon's office figuring I had about six months to live.

I don't know how others react to this kind of news. I don't know what is normal and I don't know if my feeling were typical. But I wasn't afraid or angry. I felt a great sadness. I was sad because there was so much left undone, so many things I would never see or do, and most of all I was sad over leaving my family and leaving Eileen alone in the world.

I didn't tell anyone what was going on and tried to hide my feelings, but such a burden is difficult to conceal. For the next couple of days I marched, I sat in class, I went to physical training and did my daily chores. But my mind wasn't there. I did each task without enthusiasm or feeling. I wasn't paying attention in class. I couldn't keep my mind on the required reading and study. In just three days I fell disastrously behind. But who cared? I had no future. Nothing mattered. What was the worst thing they could do to me? Kill me.

The dermatologist had said it would be three days before he would have the results of the biopsy. In three days I would know how much time I had left. In agony I waited. On the third day I couldn't stand it anymore. I slipped away to the telephone and called the dermatology department. When my doctor came on the line, he seemed surprised that I was so anxious about the results. I explained I appreciated compassion, but the truth was better; and I told him the flight surgeon had explained everything. After I finished speaking, the dermatologist said he wanted to see me that afternoon.

In his office he stated that he was the specialist—the one to believe—and once again he assured me that he had gotten the melanoma in time. I now know what it feels like to have a death sentence hanging over you and I also know the feeling of relief when that sentence is repealed. Even though I would have to have a second surgery to remove more tissue, I knew I was going to live.

Once again I was required to check in with the flight surgeon. This time he didn't say much, except a departing comment to the effect this was still serious business. "Yes, Sir," I obligingly responded, but thinking about my three days of agony, I added silently, "You jerk." I've often wondered if the flight surgeon had received a phone call from the dermatologist telling him to knock off the scare tactics.

A week later I had a follow up visit with the dermatologist. That's when the other shoe dropped. "Chuck, there is no such thing as medical certainty. I can only officially report that there is a 98%

probability that the cancer is gone. There is always a chance it could return someday." He continued, "Under the regs this condition disqualifies you for flight service." He finished, "You can appeal, but in the end you will still most likely be disqualified." So that was it. My career as a navigator was over before it began. Outwardly, I expressed disappointment. Inwardly, however, it was a relief. I had fallen behind and my enthusiasm had never fully returned.

My last day in the Air Force ended as awkwardly as my first had begun. After spending hours in lines being processed out, I was sent to a special barracks for airmen being discharged. This time, a sharp-looking airman issued me sheets and a pillow, told me to go make my bed and report for a work detail. I went upstairs, threw my sheets and duffel bag on the bed, pulled off my shoes and went to sleep. A few hours later, an airman making his rounds on fire watch saw me and ordered me to get up. I was too tired to be bothered with this nonsense. He repeated the command and I told him to "Buzz off." He scurried away and in a few minutes returned with a sergeant in tow. I could hear them whispering behind me. Then I heard the sergeant say, "Leave him alone, he's from OTS. It's rough over there."

But hey, they didn't know how rough it had been.

- 10 -

Willow Beach Again

After being discharged from the Air Force at the end of January I returned to Reno. Eileen was working as a clerk in a department store and I was once again unemployed. Still I felt lucky to be alive. Whether it had been extreme good luck or divine destiny, my circuit through the Air Force had saved my life and now I was back on track.

Vowing I would never again take my eyes off the goal of becoming a ranger, I called Bill Sherman at Lake Mead and he immediately hired me. My call to Bill came at the exact right time, because shortly before my phone call, Lake Mead had received grant money to hire fifteen backcountry rangers. Bill was looking for a backcountry ranger and I was told to report for work on March 1, 1983.

With the help of our parents, Eileen and I moved from Reno to Willow Beach. Our new home was on the grounds of the Willow Beach Fish Hatchery and I was happily back in the green and gray— back on course doing what I wanted to do.

I had been at Willow Beach less than a week when I was awakened in the middle of the night by a phone call from the park dispatcher. Still groggy with sleep I heard her say, "Chuck, we have a shooting. The reporting party is at the pay phone outside the store."

That message should have brought me fully awake, but I was living at Willow Beach, also known as "Pillow Beach" because it was a peaceful quiet place and, of course, there couldn't possibly be a shooting there. The call had to be a mistake and even though I wasn't really awake, I promised the dispatcher I would check it out.

As I drove the half-mile from the fish hatchery to the marina I wondered what this was really about. The idea that it could actually be a shooting just wasn't registering.

With exaggerated control and calmness I pulled up to the group. After all I was the law here. Whatever might have happened I could handle it. I rolled down my window and asked, "Did someone here call for a ranger?"

The answer came back immediately. "Yes, this man," pointing to a man standing beside him, "has been shot."

What? Shot! No! I instantly went from zero to one hundred on the excited scale. I grabbed the radio mic and in a voice that sounded like Mickey Mouse told the dispatcher to find Bill and get him down here—now!

The victim had been shot in the heel and calf. The spokesman for the group told me that he and his friends had been fishing from a boat a short distance downstream from Hoover Dam. They were using a bright lantern. Around 10 p.m. someone in a camp on a nearby shore called out and told them to turn off the light. The fishermen refused and a shouting match developed which ended with the threat, "Turn off the lantern or I'll shoot it out." However, the shooter was not an expert marksman, because he missed the lantern and hit one of the fishermen.

After what seemed like forever, Bill arrived. With Bill in charge, a small army of rangers and Metro Police Officers was assembled. Bill's plan was straightforward. There were only two ways out of the canyon and we would block both. Then, like marines, we would storm the beach from the river and catch the group off guard.

Everybody had a job to do. Mine was to drive the boat and once we landed, to illuminate the scene. Because the canyon was pitch-black and the river crisscrossed by treacherous sand bars, the trip up river demanded both vigilance and the careful exercise of my as yet undeveloped boating skills. However, I successfully piloted the boat to a point opposite the camp and anxiously awaited the take-down.

Bill studied the scene. Only the dying embers of the suspects' campfire could be seen and not a sound could be heard. They were apparently sleeping. After what seemed like a lifetime, Bill leaned over to me and whispered, "Let's go." I throttled forward, eyes glued on my only reference point, the embers of the campfire. Then, just off shore, I switched on the searchlight. The boat's bow hit the soft sand and slid up onto the beach, but before we had come to a complete stop, Bill and other shotgun-armed rangers were already going over the bow and fanning out with weapons pointed and shouted commands. I watched as the camp's occupants were gathered together and made to assume a prone position.

During this round-up I remained with the boat, holding the floodlight on the camp with one hand and pointing my revolver with the other. As the suspects were brought back and laid out, I looked down my sights, the deadly tool pointed at the center of a man's chest. As I look back now I find it remarkable how completely detached I was from fear. Once Bill had arrived, I regained my composure, became like a private taking an order from the general. Not until the next day when the adrenaline wore off would the thought occur that I might have killed someone. However, even then, I never entertained the thought that I could have been shot. If I had any fear at all, it was the fear that I might screw up—might let Bill down.

As it turned out, the suspects cooperated completely and, other than the stormtrooper landing, the incident was somewhat routine for Lake Mead. The men were questioned and the camp searched, but the weapon was not found and since no one could be identified as the shooter, they were all released.

This incident was not the norm for Willow Beach. While it had started out with excitement of a shooting, Willow Beach really was a quiet backwater by Lake Mead standards. It was the perfect place for a green as grass seasonal to work. Beside me, Bill had hired another rookie, Larry. Larry was also just starting his ranger career and like me, aspired to be hired on permanently. I became the backcountry ranger and Larry the front country ranger. Of course, I wouldn't have many law enforcement contacts with my remote work, but Larry was theoretically where the action was.

One afternoon as I came stomping–trying to act both busy and important–into our small, one-desk ranger station, Larry called my attention to some papers. He had a printout from dispatch that listed every ranger in the park and the citations they had issued during the last two weeks. Every ranger on the list had issued dozens of tickets except two—Chuck and Larry. We had issued no citations. Like Laurel and Hardy, we discussed what this must mean. Our conclusion was that we obviously wouldn't know a violation if it slapped us in the face. Clearly, we reasoned, we weren't doing a good job and we needed to try harder.

A few days later, as I was driving through the launch ramp parking lot, I noticed that several of the empty boat trailers didn't have license plates. Ah ha! Criminals! I summoned Larry to the scene of the crime spree. Together we proceeded around the lot and left a citation on the windshield of every offender's vehicle. When we were done, I headed home. Larry still had a few hours left on his shift.

About an hour later, Larry was banging on my front door. Excitedly he proclaimed, "We have a problem." He explained that when fishermen launched small boats, before they backed into the water, they removed their trailer lights and with them, their license plates. How did Larry know this? It had all been explained to him by a number of hip-hopping mad fishermen. All our ticketed trailers actually had license plates and an angry bunch of fishermen were demanding that we unticket them.

At the academy I had been taught how to issue tickets, but not how to unissue them. What to do? We tried to call Bill but he wasn't home. So we then tried Keith, the other permanent ranger at Willow Beach. Keith answered the phone and listened to our dilemma. With purposeful drama he said, "This is serious, but fortunately there is a procedure for canceling tickets." Then, "Is Larry there with you?"

"Yes," I replied.

"OK, then both of you raise your right hands and repeat after me, I do solemnly swear, that as a peace officer of the United States of America, I will never do anything this dumb again." With our hands in the air like a couple of idiots, we burst out laughing. It was a good lesson because I never again issued a ticket that wasn't wholly deserved.

Being the backcountry ranger was definitely the best job. The front country guys like Larry had to stick around the developed areas and deal with people problems. But my days were carefree. I came and went as I pleased. My work was a mix of patrolling and projects. Put simply, my job was to ensure that the few backcountry visitors did no harm to the desert, and the desert did no harm to them.

Because park maintenance crews rarely ventured beyond the developed areas, I patrolled the desert, replaced damaged signs, picked up litter, marked the park's boundary, and with a shovel made minor repairs to the dirt roads. Exploration was also a big part of the job. Bill insisted that a ranger should know his district like the back of his hand. Periodically Bill would schedule the park's airplane for an exploratory flight over the district. That spring on one such trip, Bill discovered a previously unknown mine in a very remote, rugged part of the district. He asked me to check it out. A few days later I reported back that I hadn't been able to find the mine so Bill decided he, Larry, and I would investigate together.

On exploration day we loaded climbing gear into Bill's Ram Charger and headed south. After a torturous drive over a long ago forgotten road we found a small, timbered shaft. The hole went straight down. We couldn't see the bottom and sounds made by rocks dropped over the edge indicated it was about a hundred feet to the floor. There were two ways down—a hoist way and a ladder way.

Since the ladder looked rotten, Bill announced that I should rappel down. I gave Bill a "Why me?" look, and he assured me that there was nothing to worry about. I geared up and Bill set the anchors and dropped the rope into the void. I was nervous, but Bill was the boss. If he said it was okay, that was good enough for me. Over the edge I went. As I dropped deeper and deeper, the rope above me created a continuous rain of dirt. I moved slowly and cautiously, fearful of dislodging rocks or timbers. At the bottom I landed in a pile of debris: rocks, timbers, tumble weeds and to my dismay, the skeletal remains of a rather large snake.

Just as I was about to call out that there might be snakes in the mine, Bill yelled down, "Hey, there's a rattlesnake up here in the ladder way." The next thing he said was even more disturbing. "Is there any place where you can get out of the shaft?"

There was a tunnel leading away from the shaft. But going into an unexplored tunnel where there might be more snakes didn't seem like a good idea. I answered that there was a tunnel, but before I could explain my reluctance, Bill yelled, "Good, get out of the shaft 'cause I'm going to shoot the snake." I scurried for cover, still thinking "this is not a good idea." The gunshot was deafening and a fine rain of dirt fell again. With ears ringing the next thing I heard was, "I missed." I thought, "Great! Now I'll be snake bit and deaf."

The snake went back into its hole and Bill belayed me as I climbed up the ladder. Back on top I thought, "Now where else could you find a job where rappelling into a snake-infested mine was part of your day?" Danger, excitement, adventure; this was my kind of job.

What made guys like Bill stand out was their old school creativity and resourcefulness. He could get things done and find new ways to make do with what was available.

For example: Willow Beach didn't have a fire truck. We needed one but the Park Service is basically a poor agency and there was no money. For most people that would have been the end of it, but not Bill. He was determined to acquire a fire truck even if he had to build one.

When the Willow Beach National Fish Hatchery purchased a new fish hauling tanker, Bill managed to convince the manager to give him the old tanker. Bill left Willow Beach with the worn-out fish hauler and after two weeks at the park welding shop returned with, well—something. It was a Rube Goldberg-looking machine. On top of the green and white cab was a hand-me-down, red bubble-gum-jar light that looked like it belonged on Dick Tracy's car. Behind the cab, and in front of the large silver water tank, Bill had mounted an old gasoline-engine-driven pump and had plumbed a spaghetti mess of shiny, new, galvanized pipes and valves to various intakes and discharge points around the truck. Down each side of the water tank were plywood boxes filled with fire hoses, and there was even a ladder on one side for good measure. It didn't exactly look like a fire truck, unless you stood at a distance, squinted and used some imagination, but Bill was rightfully proud of it and I was highly impressed. Keith made jokes, but I think he was impressed too.

Once Bill had his fire truck he had a new problem—where to put it? Willow Beach didn't have a fire station; so after some more tall-talking the maintenance man agreed to let Bill keep his fire truck in the maintenance garage. It just barely fit.

For the next few weeks we trained with the new apparatus and despite its appearance, the machine worked well. However, Bill was still possessive about his work. We were always under his watchful eye.

One morning when I came into the ranger station, Keith was sitting at the one shared desk and looking bored. Like one kid daring another, he said, "Want to go for a ride in the fire truck?"

"What about Bill?" I replied.

"He'll never know."

Inside the garage, Keith got behind the wheel. I climbed into the passenger seat. As Keith eased the big truck forward he reached out the window and flicked the rope hanging down from the roll-up door away from the truck's mirror. Just as the truck cleared the building we heard a horrible crash; the clang and wrench of metal. It sounded like the whole garage was collapsing.

The rope Keith flicked had, in strict accordance with Murphy's Law, swung around and caught on the hose box and we were now towing the sixteen foot door down the street. For a split second Keith and I looked at each other with that deer-in-the-headlights look and then started laughing. It took Keith and me most of the day to re-hang the door and pound out the dents. The door was warped and it now took someone with the strength of Hercules to roll it up, but we figured Bill might not notice it for a day or two. No such luck. The first thing he said when he came in the next morning was, "What happened to the garage door?"

I spent nearly a year at Willow Beach. But the time passed very quickly, as it does when you are happy. Bill and Keith were wonderful role models. Bill was an example of what a good ranger should be and Keith was a happy-go-lucky character that made the job fun. I worked hard, learned a lot and thoroughly enjoyed myself. But, all good things must come to an end, and so it was for my time at Willow Beach. In the fall, Bill cut my hours back in order to extend my season as long as possible.

With more time on my hands, I enrolled in an Emergency Medical Technician course at the community college in Las Vegas. Larry and I attended classes together during the day and twice a week in the evenings, Eileen and I drove to Kingman, Arizona, where I took classes to become an Arizona peace officer and Eileen took business classes at the college.

Besides taking classes, I applied for every "ranger" job or more accurately, any job on a hiring list anywhere in the country. To get hired permanently one had to get their name on a "park technician" register. These registers were maintained by the Office of Personnel Management and were periodically opened to new applicants. The trick however, was knowing when to apply since OPM wouldn't tell you when the register was open. Whenever we heard that a list opened we applied. Where in the country didn't matter, the only thing that counted was getting on a list, any list.

In December I received an early Christmas present. My name had been picked by the Army Corps of Engineers for a park technician job at Rough River Lake in Kentucky. It was a subject-to-furlough GS-4, and only paid about seven thousand dollars a year, but it was a permanent position and I took it, or more accurately, I jumped at the opportunity. I knew that once I was in the door I could then transfer over to the Park Service.

- 11 -

Rough River

In early January 1984, Eileen and I packed everything we owned into our two vehicles—a small Ford Courier pick-up and an Oldsmobile Omega sedan. We said good-bye to Willow Beach and set out on a transcontinental journey. Kentucky for us was on the far side of the moon. Neither of us had ever been that far from home and we didn't know what to expect. Because there was no fat in our budget we had only enough money to cover the fuel expenses of two vehicles on a trip of two thousand miles and to rent a house at the end of the journey. Even modest repairs to either vehicle could have siphoned off all our cash. However, with the naiveté of youth and a spirit of adventure, the problems and hazards we might encounter were cheerfully ignored. Fortunately, there were no unforeseen expenses.

To help pass the time as we traveled down Interstate 40, I kept tuning the radio to the local stations along the way. As we passed through Amarillo, Texas, there was a story on the news about a small airplane that had crashed into Lake Meredith. The newscaster mentioned that Lake Meredith was part of the National Park Service. Someday, I thought, I would be a ranger serving in one of our country's national parks. But I had never heard of Lake Meredith and I was certain my career would never take me to this obscure park in the Texas Panhandle.

At the end of five long days on the road, plus we had a day stop-over with my grandfather in Oklahoma, we arrived in Leitchfield, Kentucky. It was a small town and to my tired eyes, a depressing and rundown place. We found a cafe, but disappointment had taken away my appetite. I just kept thinking, "This is not what I expected."

There were two motels in town and we checked into the "better" one. The carpet in our room was dirty and stained; there was a puddle next to the toilet in the bathroom and the sheets that covered a sagging mattress had been washed to paper thinness. If this was the better motel, then the other one must have been a real pigsty.

After days of excitement and anticipation, my emotions crashed. I told Eileen I was going for a walk. In the evening darkness I walked around the center of town with (I'm ashamed to say) tears in my eyes. In hindsight, my feelings were grossly disproportionate to our situation, but at the time I just needed to let go.

Bright and early the next morning Eileen and I began searching for a place to live. We contacted a real estate agent who took us around town showing us houses. We quickly discovered that the only places we could afford were dilapidated house trailers and rundown shacks. After a couple of stops the real estate agent abandoned the idea of earning a commission and in an act of kindness told us he could get us into new, low income housing in a town about thirty miles away.

In a snowstorm Eileen and I moved our few belongings into an eight-unit apartment building in Hardinsburg. As we carried our things up the stairs, I watched the sheriff and mortician carry a suicide corpse out of an adjacent unit. I thought with irony, "Ah home! What a fine place it is!" Two rooms and a bathroom provided ample space for our furniture: a mattress (no bed frame), a card table, two folding metal chairs, and a milk crate stand for our 12-inch television.

As it turned out, Hardinsburg was a great place to live. It was Mayberryesque, small but full of friendly folks. Surrounding the town were farms nestled among gently rolling tree-covered hills. Ten miles away was Rough River Lake and the Army Corps of Engineers Project Office.

Initially I thought my new job as a park technician would be the same as my seasonal ranger jobs were with the Park Service. But there was very little similarity. Rangering in the Army Corps of Engineers was mostly about land issues and recreation site management. Rangers here didn't do law enforcement or emergency responses. Those things were contracted out to the local sheriff's department. The rangers at Rough River mostly oversaw the contractors who ran and maintained the campgrounds and managed the hundreds of use permits and licenses issued to the public.

The Army Corps of Engineers called Rough River a project, not a park. The project encompassed Rough River Lake and a narrow band of shoreline around it. In addition to the impounding dam, the project's only assets were several campgrounds and launch ramps. Along the boundary were over one hundred housing subdivisions. Needless to say, long stretches of the boundary were lined with homes and vacation cabins. The Corps allowed the owners of those homes to have boat docks on the lake and stairways down to them. The most amazing thing to me was that the Corps also allowed homeowners to clear the trees and brush away and plant lawns on the land below their houses. Coming from a "Preserve and Protect" philosophy of the National Park Service, I found all this use and disturbing of natural vegetation to be alien.

My job was to assist the project's two rangers, Carlie and Stan, in managing and monitoring all of this use. I spent much of the late winter and spring learning my new job and following Carlie around as he conducted business. I also made a good-faith attempt to fit into the community by joining the Hardinsburg Volunteer Fire Department. But I found Kentucky to be a foreign land and the Corps a poor substitute for the Park Service.

Fortunately, when summer arrived Carlie gave me a plum assignment. I was to check the entire project boundary—all several hundred miles of it—and locate any unauthorized and unlicensed structures encroaching on government land. This assignment would keep me busy for most of the summer. It was a blessing, because I hated office and clerk work.

The project's boundary was set on an elevation contour in most places. Therefore, from a known lake elevation I could measure up the slope the required height and locate the boundary. Because the lake was long and snaked around, almost like a river, the best way to check for encroachments was by boat. Every day a seasonal park technician and I would launch our small johnboat, travel by water to the day's work site and walk the boundary documenting any encroachments.

One sunny, hot day a funny thing happened—a perfect example of my inexperience and naiveté. When we boated up to the shore at a new subdivision I saw what I was certain was an encroachment. The shoreline here sloped up from the water in a long gentle grade and at the crest of the hill several hundred yards away was a two-story house. After several weeks on the job I had a good eye for the boundary. I knew the house was on private land but down the hill from it were several rabbit hutches and a large garden. These were too low. They were on project land.

Our method of determining elevation was crude but it worked. Using a handheld telescope level, and by knowing my eye height, I could work my way up a slope in a series of lifts until I reached the elevation that marked the project's boundary.

Using this method to establish elevation, I worked my way up the slope with my helper following along behind me. The garden was well below the boundary, but that was okay—homeowners could clear brush and plant lawns—I saw no difference between planting a lawn and planting a garden. Without breaking concentration I continued to work my way up, walking between the rows of plants. At the top of the garden I reached the real prize I was after. The rabbit hutches were indeed on the project. Sometimes we would toil and sweat for days without finding a single encroachment, consequently when we did discover something it was like a small victory.

Pleased with myself I turned to tell my helper what we had found, but he was gone. He had not followed me through the garden and was now, in fact, all the way back down the slope by the boat. I yelled and waved for him to come up. He yelled and waved for me to come down. Then a woman wearing a frumpy housedress yelled from the second floor porch of the house, "Who are you? What ya doing down thar?"

In my best authoritative voice I yelled back, "I'm with the Army Corps of Engineers and we have a problem here! Your rabbit hutches are on government property!" The woman didn't seem to understand so I yelled again, "Your rabbit hutches are on government property. You'll have to move them."

She again demanded to know what I was doing and I explained again and added that I would be sending her a letter. Having done my duty I turned and marched back down the hill, through the garden to the boat. That's when my helper explained that what I had thought was a garden was actually a field of marijuana.

The absurdity of a uniformed government official, standing in the middle of a marijuana field, demanding that an illegal rabbit hutch be moved or there would be hell to pay was too much. My helper chuckled and I laughed until my eyes watered.

Rough River Lake was beautiful. My boss, Carlie, was as fine a man as you will ever meet, but I was not really happy in my work. The Corps was just not the Park Service. So when my ninety-day probation period was up I began applying for jobs with the Park Service. Keith from Willow Beach sent me the Service's job vacancy list every two weeks. I applied for every GS-5 ranger job on the list.

One day while working in the office I got a telephone call from the Chief Ranger at Independence Hall in Philadelphia. He was prepared to offer me a job, but before I accepted he described the living conditions in the area and explained that if I took the position I would have to promise him I would stay for at least one year. Independence was an urban park in downtown Philadelphia. There was no affordable place to live close by and the job was just a glorified security guard, rattling doors and walking a beat. I knew I could not promise him a year. My dad had taught me that a man's word was his bond and while a few months was one thing, a year or more was too much for me. Sadly, I declined the offer. As I hung up the phone I couldn't help but wonder if I hadn't just made the biggest mistake of my life. Would there ever be another offer?

But, a few weeks later on a hot, humid Friday afternoon near the end of July, Eileen and I decided to go out to the project and explore some caves Carlie had told me about. Our first stop was the local mercantile to buy Eileen a pair of coveralls. A little old lady tottered over to us as we came in. When I explained Eileen needed the coveralls for cave exploration the old woman shook her head and said, "You ought to be fishing." She thought cave exploration was foolish, but fishing was a worthwhile pastime.

As she talked I studied the store. Time had skipped over this place. It looked pretty much as it had fifty years before. While Eileen selected and paid for her coveralls, I wondered what changes I might experience in the next fifty years. How long would I live in this Norman Rockwell town? Would I ever get a job with the Park Service?

Our next stop was the Project Office to borrow a couple of flashlights. As soon as I walked in, Lindy, the secretary, announced that someone from Lake Meredith Recreation Area had called asking for me. She thought they wanted to offer me a job and she told me I must call him back right away if I wanted the job because there would be a hiring freeze on Monday. This was Friday and of course they couldn't get hold of me because we didn't have a phone. It was a luxury Eileen and I couldn't afford on my small salary.

Lake Meredith, where was that? I had heard the name somewhere but I couldn't place it. Ordinarily I would have known all about Lake Meredith from the job vacancy announcement. However, I hadn't seen the announcement. I had simply sent in an application after seeing the job listed on one of the lists that Keith had sent me. I had been shot-gunning out applications for several months in the hope that something would come up.

Excitedly, I called the number Lindy gave me. I was connected with the Chief Ranger, who explained they were prepared to offer me a GS-5 Park Ranger job. This was it! I had finally made it, a permanent position with the National Park Service. Chief Ranger Larry went on to say that he'd like to give me time to think it over, but because Ronald Reagan was freezing all hiring on Monday. He needed my answer now. This was not a problem. I blurted out, "I'll take it!"

It was only after I accepted the job that I learned the details. It was not your typical ranger job. I would be a full-time boating officer. There was no park housing, and Lake Meredith was in the Texas Panhandle. None of these facts concerned me, even though I had always pictured myself in places like Grand Teton, or Glacier, or Grand Canyon; Lake Meredith at that moment sounded just as wonderful.

After I hung up the phone I stood there in disbelief. A freeze on all government hiring was beginning on Monday. Had Eileen and I not decided to go caving, had we not stopped at the office for flashlights, I would not have received the message to call Lake Meredith in time.

As I replayed the phone call over in my head it came to me; Lake Meredith was the park where a plane had crashed when I was driving through Amarillo. I remembered a newscaster had mentioned Lake Meredith National Recreation Area and I had wondered what kind of park was located in the Texas Panhandle. Once again my life seemed to follow a circular path. I'm always going somewhere, but that place is often back where I started. Were these coincidences, luck, or something else?

During our time in Kentucky, Eileen had once again been a trouper. She was bored while I was off working and she had her own dreams that were going unaddressed, but she didn't complain. That spring we had come to the obvious conclusion that there was no telling when or where I would end up. Therefore it made no sense to wait until I settled down for her to begin her dream of law school. She had spent some of her ample idle time applying to various law schools. Several accepted her, but after careful thought she picked the University of Minnesota, in Minneapolis. Both her school and my new job would begin in September. The plan was that I would take her to Minneapolis, return to Hardinsburg, pack up and move to Texas.

- 12 -

Welcome to Lake Meredith

I was weary. I had been on the road for a week—zigzagging up and down the country for a total of more than 3,000 miles. First Eileen and I had traveled south from Hardinsburg, Kentucky, to McAlester, Oklahoma, and dropped her car off with my grandfather. Next, we turned back north, traveling to Minneapolis where Eileen would be going to school. I helped her get settled into her dorm room. Then I returned to Hardinsburg, checked out with the Corps, packed up, and now I was nearing my destination in Texas.

Lake Meredith Recreation Area is located in the panhandle of Texas, about forty miles north of Amarillo and Interstate 40. The land is flat, treeless, and empty. After leaving the Interstate, I passed a few dry-land farms but further north the land changed from grasslands into a mesquite-dotted prairie. I saw an occasional ranch building and here and there an oil well.

I came to a town called Borger. According to my map, Borger was about twenty miles from Lake Meredith. The town was dominated by the oil industry and literally stunk. I thought, "Glad I don't have to live here."

Continuing on, I began to wonder if my map was correct. Parks, in my experience, were associated with beauty—spectacular mountains, deep canyons, virgin forests. But here there were only low rolling hills, actually just small undulations in the flat plain. Studding the landscape were rocking horse oil well pumps and batteries of small, steel tanks. The ground around these tanks was stained black from countless oil spills, and linking all of these grimy places were dozens of crisscrossing dirt roads. I thought, "I can't be close, this place is too damned ugly."

And then moments later, as the narrow two-lane highway crested a rise, I saw it. Lake Meredith was a pretty, blue lake, filling a shallow, wide canyon in an otherwise flat, featureless plain. It was no Grand Canyon, but it was my new home.

Flowing across the flat plain, known as the Llana Estacado, the Canadian River had over thousands of years of erosion created a canyon. Lake Meredith now filled the bottom of that canyon and the shoreline in most places rose steeply from the water to the plain above. Except for a few cottonwood trees in the bottoms of side canyons, the main vegetation was bunch grasses and thorny mesquites.

Lake Meredith Recreation Area is a relatively small park. The lake, created by an earthen dam on the Canadian River, is approximately ten miles long and less than a mile wide. The boundary of the park is generally less than a mile from the water's edge. Normally, Lake Meredith would have been an unlikely candidate for inclusion in the National Park system, but it was the only significantly large tract of public land within hundreds of miles. Because this was the only area available in the panhandle for outdoor recreation it had been designated a National Recreation Area. Without scenery, Lake Meredith was all about fun on the water.

I drove to the headquarters located outside of the park in the small town of Fritch. I checked in and met my boss, Chief Ranger Larry, a tall, middle-aged man with a soft, gentle voice.

Introductions over, the next order of business was finding a place to live. My options were once again controlled by my bank account. After a short hunt I located a one-bedroom apartment in Buena Vista, just outside Borger. The building had been thrown up during the previous boom times in the oil patch and little consideration had been given to anything but plain, basic shelter. It was ugly and it stunk. But it was cheap and with Eileen away at law school, I would basically be a bachelor for the next three years. Contrary to my earlier assessment, I was glad to find something I could afford. Since I owned next to nothing, it took me less than an hour to move in.

Lake Meredith, in terms of administration, was unique. The park was divided into four districts. The Sanford-Yake District was the front country or developed area. It was in this district where most of the park visitation was concentrated. It included a life-guarded swimming beach and picnic area below the Sanford Dam, two primitive and two developed campgrounds, three launch ramps, a marina, ranger station and the maintenance facilities. Two of the other districts were more or less backcountry districts. One was primarily the north side of the lake and the other was the river bottom upstream from the lake. The final district, the one to which I was assigned, was the Lake District. It was the lake itself. Technically I had no responsibility for anything not on or in the water.

John, the Lake District Ranger, was my boss. It was his job to supervise me and two summer seasonal rangers. Together we patrolled the lake, enforced boating regulations, investigated boating and swimming accidents, assisted the boating public, and when needed, conducted search and rescue operations. For these duties we had a fleet of three patrol boats. Given that the lake was the main draw for visitors, the Lake District was a major player in the park's operations.

By the time I reported for duty in September, the busy summer season was already over and the summer seasonal rangers had all returned to their schools, either as students or teachers. During my first few weeks I spent most of my time becoming oriented to the park.

I remember one particular fall day because that was the day I learned an important lesson. I've learned many things about my job by experience—the school of hard knocks. But this was one time when I listened and learned. It was a stormy day and I stood by the window of the ranger station looking out at gunmetal gray clouds and listening to the wind howling around the eaves of the building. Since arriving at Lake Meredith I had only been out on the lake a few times, and only during times of calm weather. Speaking almost to myself, I said, "Today is no day to be on the lake." From across the room, a chair creaked and the long-time Sandford-Yake ranger Bob said, "Now is exactly the time when you should be on the water. You go out when others come in."

I remember Bob's exact words, because I felt he was somebody to trust. Bob had been a school teacher and was a part-time ranger. He'd worked at Lake Meredith for many years and he had a good story to tell for every occasion. He was Mr. Lake Meredith Ranger and even looked the part. Not because he was overly handsome or physically fit—for he was a graying, middle-aged man of large stature and girth—but because he looked fatherly, kind, wise, and capable. He had seen it all and done it all. So if Bob said go out into the storm then that was the thing to do.

Bob's comment about being proactive was a lesson that I would never forget. My job, beyond protecting the resource, was to serve others and not just when it was convenient and the winds were calm. That day I didn't jump up and head for the boats, for I was far too inexperienced to go out on my own, but I thought about Bob's words and remembered them.

A few evenings later, as I was washing my supper dishes, the phone rang. It was my boss John. He told me there was an overdue fisherman and asked me to meet him at the ranger station. My reaction was a surge of excitement and a feeling of "Oh boy, my first search and rescue mission!"

An hour later, John and I were underway in the heavy-hulled aluminum *Monark* patrol boat. It had a decked-over bow and a four-rung ladder connected it with the cockpit behind and below it.

We slowly probed our way up lake, roughly paralleling the shoreline, checking each cove and side canyon. The shoreline was a silent blackness which swallowed up all light and there was no moon. The stars twinkled brightly, causing small ripples on the lake to shimmer like silver.

Still unfamiliar with the lake, I was unaware that the water was changing as we drew near the upsteam end of the lake. Where the Canadian River dumped into Lake Meredith, it also dumped silt. Literally millions of cubic yards of New Mexico were slowly filling the lake. At the upper reaches of the lake—beginning over a mile offshore—the water becoming shallow, turned chocolate brown and gradually thickened until it became land. Just like flypaper, the brown ooze would stick a boat fast if one ventured too far. John knew of this danger and he also knew how far we could travel safely.

Unaware of the mud hazard, I stood at the foot of the bow ladder straining to see through the darkness. Intent on showing John that I was a good and dependable hand, every muscle was taut in anticipation of action. I was all business. Then suddenly BAAAA! The nastiest horn I have ever heard split the night. My reaction was instinctive. In my high school biology class it was called "fight or flight" and I chose flight. Like a coiled spring being released, I launched straight up, and without the benefit of the ladder, landed on the bow deck. I was on my way to abandoning ship when John's laughter stopped me.

The alarm was the engine's overheating warning. The silty water had caused the motor to run hot. Prior to my embarrassing leap, I had not even known boat motors had such alarms. I had a lot to learn. As for our fisherman, on our return trip down the other side of the lake we found him patiently waiting on the shore for the Park Service to come looking for him.

Because I was a rookie, I couldn't be turned loose on my own. This was a problem for the park. Rangers work independently and have to be able to deal with a wide variety of situations. They are teachers and cops, rescuers of man or beast, firefighters, and handymen. Chief Ranger Larry was painfully aware of my shortcomings and he wasted no time in beginning my education. Larry knew he had only the fall and winter to get ready for the always busy spring and summer visitor seasons.

Even before I arrived, Larry had enrolled me in a SCUBA class. Being a water park with a small staff, Larry needed all fit hands to be on the SCUBA diving team. Throughout September and October I attended classes at the YMCA pool in Amarillo. In November, the class held its graduation and check-out dives at the Blue Hole in Santa Rosa, New Mexico.

The Blue Hole was like a giant well, almost fifty feet in diameter and about eighty feet deep. The water was crystal clear and warm, even though the air above was freezing. At the time I didn't know that this would be the last time in my diving career that I would swim in such ideal conditions.

Shortly after I became a certified diver, I was introduced to the not so ideal conditions of Lake Meredith. Near the end of November, a visitor reported that while he was camped at Cedar Canyon he saw a man walk out to the end of the boat dock and throw a handgun into the lake. After taking the report, John decided that we should dive and recover the weapon. We were certain it had been used in a crime.

All of my SCUBA diving to this point had been in a controlled environment and in a wet suit. However, Lake Meredith's dive team didn't use wet suits because the lake was too cold in the winter. The dive team used dry suits. The difference between the two is huge. A wet suit is a tight-fitting neoprene suit that traps a layer of water against the skin. The diver's body heat warms the water which provides some insulation against the water outside. A dry suit on the other hand is like a space suit; a watertight, loose fitting, toasty-warm, dry capsule. As nice as it is, it does have its own set of special issues. The air inside the suit has to be regulated. As the diver goes deeper more air must be injected into the suit to combat the increasing water pressure. As the diver surfaces, air has to be released from the suit to keep it from over expanding in the decreasing pressure. A diver who is not careful can get into trouble with a dry suit. In the worst case, a diver could surface too fast, like a rising balloon, which could be fatal.

John gave me a twenty-minute briefing on the dry suit and ended his speech with the admonishment, "Remember, not too much air in the suit or you'll come to the surface like a Polaris missile."

This was to be my first real dive mission, which in itself would be cause for some apprehension. But to make matters worse, I would be using a dry suit for the first time, the visibility underwater would be about a foot, and I would be alone!

Lake Meredith's dive team used a technique called "one diver down." Most SCUBA diving is done in pairs. Divers normally use the buddy system for safety. But problems of coordination, communications and limited visibility make this practice awkward and inefficient for search and rescue. With the one-diver-down system, the diver is tethered by a line to a tender on shore. By using a system of tugs on the line the tender can communicate with and control the diver. The diver swims back and forth in a series of arcs. At the completion of each arc the tender lets out a predetermined length of line and the diver swims back on a new pass further out. The diver's safety buddy remains on the surface, suited up and ready to go in the event of a problem.

I sat down on the end of the dock and let my legs dangle in the water. The feeling was strange. The water pressing on my legs was neither wet nor cold; it only had weight. I was just getting used to this strange new sensation and concentrating on everything I needed to remember, when John slapped my tank to draw my attention. I hadn't been aware of John speaking to me and the only words I caught were his last, "Ok, let's do it."

With the grace of a rock, I leaned forward and dropped into the lake. But I didn't sink; in fact, I floated on top of the water like a water bug. The air in the suit buoyed me up. I thrashed my way to the starting point. Taking one final look back at John standing on the end of the dock, I wished he was in the water and I was up there.

Remembering his words, "Ok, let's do it," I put the regulator in my mouth, opened my suit air release valve and slowly the water rose across the glass in front of my face mask. Down I sank.

As I descended I had the feeling of walking further and further into a cave. At first I could see several feet though everything was tinted green. But gradually the water darkened and thickened until it was a dark brown haze. Looking up I could see that it was lighter, looking down it was darker, but other than that I could see nothing. Holding a hand up in front of my face mask I could only make out a ghostly shadow of the black glove. The only sound in this empty world was my heavy breathing—the sucking hiss of the regulator as I inhaled and gurgling bubbles as I exhaled.

The water was now squeezing me from every direction. My depth and air pressure gauges were on the end of a short hose. I held them up to get a reading. In the murk I couldn't read the numbers. After pressing gauges up against my mask I saw that I was only about twenty feet down. I needed to add air to my suit but how much? What if I over inflated it? John's briefing, I now realized, was entirely unsatisfactory. With great apprehension I pressed the inflation valve. Air hissed into the suit. Immediately I felt relief from the crushing weight of the water. Not too much, I thought, and I cut off the air.

I continued to drop a few more feet until I felt the bottom. It was hard, rocky and uneven, yet also covered by a thick layer of silt and slime. Whenever I touched bottom a huge cloud of brown fog boiled up and enveloped me. Outside the cloud I could see a few inches; inside it I could see nothing.

Standing still on the bottom I became aware of how tense I was. The only exposed parts of my skin were my cheeks and lips. They were numb with cold, yet inside the suit I could feel the sweat running down my back and I was breathing much too fast. "Slow, slow," I silently repeated until my breaths became more normal. I told myself, "You're here to do a job. Do it and then you can go up."

Then reminding myself of John's words, "Ok, let's do it" I began swimming my search arcs. I kept my tether taut and like a blind man felt my way along the bottom, sweeping my hands through the muck. At the end of my first pass I felt the tugs on the line telling me to stop, move out and begin working back. Visibility on the return trip was down to zero. My first pass had stirred up the silt and only by touching the bottom could I tell up from down. It was disorienting. I felt trapped and claustrophobic. Diving during training had been exciting, like flying underwater. This was terrifying. Intellectually I knew I could surface and escape this misery and nobody would say anything. But emotionally that wasn't an option. I had to do this job. I had to prove to my peers, and more importantly to myself, that I could control my fears and do what needed to be done.

I worked my way back through the brown cloud and completed the second pass. For these first arcs I had been like a lobster crawling along the bottom. There had to be a better way. I was slightly negatively buoyant which held me down. But, I reasoned, if I was neutrally buoyant I could hover just above the bottom and not stir up so much silt. I injected some air into the suit and just as planned I was able to float in the water, neither moving up nor down. Off I started again, only this time I drifted over the bottom like a dirigible over land. This new technique seemed to help. I was stirring up less fog, and I was not so terrified because my mind was occupied with the task of maintaining my balance.

And then disaster struck. Without realizing it I let my feet rise higher than my head. Before I recognized the danger the air in my suit flowed toward my feet. Suddenly I found myself hanging upside down, as if hanging from a clothes line by my feet. This was a problem John had failed to mention. I attempted to pull my feet down and discovered I couldn't. A wave of panic surged through me and with adrenaline induced strength I pumped my legs and clawed the water. Like a beetle trying to turn over, I ungracefully righted myself. What the hell had I been thinking when I told the Chief I could be a diver? At this rate, I might not survive my first mission.

With my composure regained, I continued on with the search. Several passes later, as I ran my hand over the bottom, I felt something. Fumbling in the fog I could tell it wasn't a rock. Then I recognized it—a revolver. Thank you, Lord! I signaled through the tether and started up. On my way up all my fears disappeared. How quickly things change. Now I felt the giddiness that comes from the release of great tension. I also felt the pride of a job well done.

As it would turn out, the revolver was not part of some great crime. It was just a worthless and unwanted weapon, thrown in the lake as a poor method of disposal.

Near the end of November I began counting the days and hours until Eileen flew back from Minneapolis for her Christmas break. While we had been apart before, this had been the longest separation yet. Our reunion was wonderful. Being back together made up for the fact that we had next to nothing and Christmas was going to be very lean. Law school was taking every penny we had and my lowly GS-5 salary didn't go very far. In fact I had been living pretty much on crackers and peanut butter. We couldn't afford a Christmas tree, but it didn't dampen our holiday spirit. We used ribbon taped to a wall in the shape of a tree as our tree and each of us placed our gift to the other beneath it. It was a fine holiday.

- 13 -

The Academy

The first of January spelled big doings. Eileen returned to law school and I was sent to law enforcement school. With only six field rangers, Lake Meredith could not afford anything less than full performance from all hands. Therefore, to get me up to speed, the Chief somehow maneuvered my name to the top of the Southwest Region's priority list for the Federal Law Enforcement Training Center, or FLETC, in Glynco, Georgia.

FLETC is the law enforcement academy every law enforcement ranger must attend in order to be fully commissioned. Since everyone (except the FBI) in federal law enforcement from the Library of Congress police to the U.S. Marshals is required to receive this training there is a waiting list and I was very fortunate to get into a class early in my career.

FLETC had at one time been a Naval Air Station, so it was no surprise that it looked very much like a military base. Upon my arrival I discovered no expenses had been spared in its conversion into a law enforcement academy. The old runways had been turned into driving courses for pursuit driving training. There were indoor and outdoor shooting ranges, a huge athletic complex for physical conditioning, as well as classrooms, dorms, dining halls, and all the typical infrastructure of a large college campus. But the most interesting parts of the center were the scenario training areas. Large areas of the old base housing neighborhoods had been turned into mock towns. These towns were complete with actors playing the parts of criminals, witnesses, and victims.

FLETC may have looked like a college campus, but it was run like a military boot camp and the challenges were both mental and physical. Students wore uniforms, stood for inspections, and marched. And, unlike college, failure here didn't mean a lower GPA or a do-over; failure meant unemployment. If you didn't satisfactorily pass every element, you were sent home. I didn't intend to take any chances. I hit the books hard. Fortunately, my roommate, Costa, was also a serious student and we got along great. Neither of us had a vehicle so we were stuck at the Training Center on the weekends, unless we could bum a ride with someone else. As a result of our ample time for study, Costa and I vied back and forth for top student in our class.

Everything was going well until two weeks before graduation. I had excelled in everything. I was number one in my class academically. I had earned expert marksman on the range. I had passed all my driving, physical fitness, and defensive tactics tests, as well as patrol practicals. All that remained was night revolver qualification, when disaster struck. In one of the last defensive tactics sessions, an overly exuberant classmate flipped me hard in a takedown. I landed on the floor shoulder first and suffered a painful shoulder injury. The base physician put my right arm in a sling and gave me some pills.

When I left the infirmary I knew the situation was very bad. How could I pass the night revolver qualification with my right arm strapped to my side? If I failed, I would be dismissed from the academy. FLETC gave no excused passes for such events. It was simply do or die.

I had a week to prepare for the qualification test. Of course I hoped my shoulder would heal, but after a couple of days it became obvious I wouldn't be out of the sling in time for the test. Therefore, I began practicing drawing and firing without using my right hand. I would reach across my body and pull the revolver from its holster with my left hand. Then I had to transfer the gun to my right hand, reposition my left hand on the grip, point, aim, and fire. The process was awkward and time consuming. And the qualification test was timed. But drawing and firing with my left hand was my only option, so I practiced over and over.

On the day of the qualification the instructor told me he didn't think I could pass, but he also knew what was on the line for me. My classmates were rooting for me. The start and stop of each round of fire was signaled by a whistle. When the whistle blew I would reach across, draw, hold, reposition, aim and fire. Time after time, my last shot rang out just as the cease fire whistle would sound. In retrospect this coincidence seems unlikely. I wonder if our instructor didn't have something to do with my passing. Nevertheless I did pass.

Two days before graduation I was called out of class and told my grandfather had died. I had completed all my requirements, so the academy agreed to let me leave early and made the necessary arrangements. While I would have liked to have gone through the graduation ceremony with my classmates, I felt a stronger drive to be with my dad and family during this time of sorrow.

After the funeral I returned to a quiet, lonesome routine at Lake Meredith. Eileen was gone, my home buddy Kit Carson, our cat, was still with my parents in Nevada (where I had sent her while I was in the academy) and outside of my co-workers, I had no friends in the area.

Without any reason to be home, I began spending more and more time at work. I came in early and stayed late and then I began coming in on my days off. Before long I was putting in sixty, seventy, and eighty hours a week. Some of the extra time was unproductive fooling around, but most was useful labor. I worked on our boats and I cleaned and organized everything. I think I drove my peers crazy with my incessant moving things, painting things, inventorying things. But the Ranger Division benefited from my hyperactivity and when Eileen came home for the summer I spent more time with her and less time at the park.

- 14 -

In Over My Head

One morning late in April when I checked in at the ranger station, I received a message that the Chief wanted to see me. As I drove to headquarters in Fritch I kept thinking, "What does he want now?" I knew Chief Ranger Larry was trying to get me up to speed as quickly as possible, so I guessed he probably had another training class lined up for me.

Larry's office was furnished with his desk, a table, a chair for visitors, and a couple of file cabinets. Except for family photographs on his desk, little had been done to personalize the room. The man and his office were strictly about the job. This was a place where park business was conducted with little or no fanfare.

The Chief greeted me, motioned me to the visitor's chair and getting right to the point said in his soft, matter-of-fact voice, "I'm temporarily promoting you to Lake District Ranger."

My unspoken reaction was, "Wow! How did this happen?" With my time away at FLETC, I had only actually, physically been in the park for about five months. I had yet to experience anything remotely resembling the busy season, and in fact, hadn't even visited all areas of the park. In spite of my inexperience, the Chief was putting me in charge of two seasonal rangers, three patrol boats, and everything that happened on the water.

Larry explained that the Sanford-Yake District Ranger had suddenly and without forewarning quit. My boss, John Batzer, had been temporarily reassigned to take over the Sanford-Yake District and now Larry was briefing me on my new role as Lake District Ranger.

My first reaction to this news was both surprise and excitement—followed by anxiety. It wasn't that I didn't think that I could handle the job. Actually, in my ignorance, I felt I could deal with just about anything. No, my anxiety came from the realization that I didn't know what the job was or what to expect. Like a soldier going into battle for the first time, I felt ready but anxious about what was to come and how I would perform. I had never supervised anyone or managed any program. My own boating skills were still in their infancy and my knowledge of the lake was limited. This would be my first summer and ideally I should have been under someone else's guidance, but now I was to be a leader not a follower.

While I think Larry saw potential in me, his catapulting me into leadership was an act of desperation on his part. He had no one else to call upon. I was willing to bet Larry was also feeling some anxiety. In fact, he probably prayed for good luck—a quiet summer with no major problems.

As I've already said, Lake Meredith was where folks came to have fun in and on the water. Swimming, boating, water skiing, and sailing were the purposes of their visits. They were largely families and groups of friends, but there were always a few yahoos who arrived with too much alcohol. Most of the problems—fights, accidents, and fatalities—had alcohol as a major contributing factor.

These summer-fun visitors started coming to the lake as soon as the weather turned warm and by Memorial Day weekend it was a very busy place. The hotter the weather, the busier the lake became, hitting a peak of use and craziness on Fourth of July weekend. It stayed busy through July, but by August it became too dang hot and visitation began to fade. Labor Day signaled the end of the summer madness. After that final weekend people had other places to be and things to do and the lake became quiet. The typical visitor during the fall, winter, and early spring was a fishermen, hunter, or occasional day cruiser.

Just prior to Memorial Day weekend, my two seasonal rangers showed up. Nancy, a college student, had worked at Lake Meredith before as an interpreter and John Batzer had selected her for boats, based on the good job she had done for Alibetes ranger Ed. She was squared away, a hard worker, and highly dependable. My other seasonal, Mark, had also been at Lake Meredith the previous season, but in time I would learn he was not ranger material. He was immature and far from dependable.

In the few days we had before the big weekend I concentrated on preparing my staff and our equipment. I formed Nancy and Mark into a crew of two with early morning duties that included cleaning and servicing the boats before going out on the water for patrol. I would come on duty at mid-day and start patrolling in a second boat. During the busiest part of the day we would have two boats on the lake. After Mark and Nancy went home I would stay out until after dark. One of the things I had learned from Bill Sherman was that a ranger belongs in the field.

Now, to the uninitiated, boat patrol probably sounds like cushy duty. And while I found the work interesting and enjoyable most of the time, and even downright exciting at times, it could also be boring. It was never cushy. In winter, the cold, damp air cut to the bone. In summer, sweat covered your body, stung your eyes, and the sun's glare on the water forced you to squint even when wearing sunglasses. And the incessant noise and the motion could drive every ounce of energy from your body. Many a day after a full shift on the water, I walked down the gangway glad to get back on land again. Even on quiet days there was always work: servicing equipment, polishing brightwork, fixing the never-ending breakdowns, and malfunctions.

My first Memorial Day weekend lived up to the break-room war stories. It was crazy. There were people everywhere, no parking places on land, and boats swarming over the lake like water bugs on a stagnant pond. Larry had put all hands on mandatory twelve-hour shifts and still we needed more people on duty. The land rangers raced from call to call. Nancy, Mark, and I talked to boaters on the water, inspected their equipment, enforced the rules, and towed them home when their boats pooped out. But luckily we didn't have any major incidents. If indeed Larry had prayed for luck, his prayers were being answered.

After that initial surge the weeks following Memorial Day seemed routine. In fact, things were going so well I started to feel a little cocky. I actually began to believe I knew what I was doing. Only one thing troubled me—Mark. I kept receiving unofficial reports about his immaturity and lack of professionalism, but these rumors were never enough to act on. Nancy, who worked with him and would know what was going on, never said a word.

This was my first experience with government bureaucracy and I was amazed and overwhelmed at the amount of paperwork. There was paperwork for everything. Gas up a boat—paperwork. Write a ticket—more paperwork. Talk to a visitor—even this had to be noted on a form. Order supplies—write requisitions and justifications. Conduct training—make a record for the files. If you made an arrest or investigated an accident the paperwork could take hours, and if someone died it could take days.

As the days counted down to the Fourth of July weekend, both the temperature and visitation continued to climb. The Sanford-Yake land rangers were busy on weekends in the late afternoons rushing from call to call. Drunks here, car wrecks there. Activity on the water also increased but we had yet to deal with anything really serious.

Then came Fourth of July weekend! From the time I began my shift each day until I threw in the towel some twelve hours later, I raced from boating violations to boat accidents to boat tows to disorderly drunks without a break. But finally, the long weekend of craziness came to an end. There had been a few visitors injured and a few had gone to jail, but no fatalities. Everyone from the Chief on down breathed a sigh of relief. We had made it. The worse was over; soon summer would begin its slow withdrawal.

Then a couple of days later I found out just how bad the worst could be. The day started out as usual. Before leaving the apartment I stopped in front of the mirror to check my uniform. I adjusted my shiny gold badge and whistled, "Hi-Ho, Hi-Ho, it's off to work I go." Feeling great, I stepped out the door and clattered down the stairs to my parking space. This was how I went to work each day—whistling and singing. That day was no different.

It was a fifteen-mile drive to work. In the town of Sanford I turned a corner at a four-way stop for the last leg of my commute and I found myself looking at two ambulances, two patrol vehicles with lights flashing, and several other cars. In the center of the road an officer was directing traffic. I took a second look and I recognized the officer was Nancy. I pulled over and Nancy came running and shouting, "There's been a terrible accident." She pointed as she ran and explained how this boat ran over a person from that boat and... How could a boat run over someone on a street corner? I held up my hand, stopped her disjointed description and asked her to explain it all again.

She began once more, "Not here." Then explained that the accident was on the lake and the paramedics from Borger had met them here and the accident victim was being transferred to the ambulance.

She explained that two family groups had been boating and towing water skiers. The victim, a little girl of about eleven years, had fallen and as her parents were circling back to pick her up a second boat with a father towing his son on skies ran directly over her. The little girl's parents had watched helplessly as the horror unfolded.

The ambulance took off with lights flashing and siren on. I told Nancy to go to the hospital, find out the status of the victim, and comfort her parents. I took the operator of the other boat—a man clearly distraught and close to tears—with me to the ranger station.

At the station I directed the man to follow me down to the basement break room and offered him a cup of coffee in a feeble attempt to calm his fears. When he seemed ready I asked if he could tell me what happened. He nodded, but when I began to read him his "rights" tears welled up in his eyes.

We were well into the interview when the phone rang. It was Nancy. She paused and then said, "The little girl died." Oh God! I turned my back to the father who was searching for hope in my words and an expression of relief in my eyes. I couldn't let him see the horror I felt. Nancy hung up. I held the phone for a moment longer, pretending to still be listening, while I regained my composure. I finally turned around and said without emotion, "She died." The man began to sob. As I watched his uncontrolled outpouring of grief I thought, "Why do these things happen? A family is forever damaged and a man is forever changed." Now I knew how bad the worst could be.

The death of that child had a deeper impact on me than I was willing to admit. Consequently, a few days later when I came to work and found Mark up to his usual immature behavior, my pent-up grief found an opportune target.

Nancy and Mark were in the ranger station "practicing" their take down and handcuffing techniques. At least that was how it had started, but by the time I walked in, Mark had pinned Nancy's arms behind her back and she was struggling to get free. Bob, the district ranger from the north side of the lake, was sitting at his desk nearby and looking on disapprovingly. As I came through the door I heard Nancy say, "I give, that hurts."

That was it. I snapped. "Okay, my turn, cuff me," I ordered Mark. He hesitated. I was fresh out of the academy, I was fit, and I was angry. I countered Mark's move, had his hand behind his back before he realized what was happening. I slammed him into the wall, drove him to the ground, and landed on his back. It was over in seconds. Of course, I knew I shouldn't have done it, but it felt good. I looked back over my shoulder expecting disapproval, but both Nancy and Bob were grinning. While I don't recommend this type of behavior toward subordinates, in this case it had the desired effect. Mark's behavior around me improved after that.

The remainder of the summer was relatively quiet. It took days to complete the investigation of the tragic accident because I knew I had to get it right: for justice for the little girl's parents and fairness to the man that killed her. In the fall, under the Chief's guidance, I presented a manslaughter case to the Grand Jury in Amarillo. They eventually ruled, "no bill."

The summer of 1985 was in many regards the beginning of my career. It wasn't the beginning that I had imagined for myself, but it was a solid and fair beginning. For the most part I had done well, although some areas, such as my supervision skills, needed more work. What I had lacked in know-how I made up for in drive and hard work. The Lake District finished up the season with good statistics. Our patrol hours were up. Our contacts were up and with the exception of the one fatality, we had a good season accident-wise. However, being lucky had more to do with the outcome than being good. If I ever had a chance to be the district ranger again, I knew I would do better.

- 15 -

Winter

Even before the cool days of autumn arrived, the Chief was once again focused on my education and development. A park ranger, especially in a small park, has to be proficient in many areas. The typical park ranger is not only the "sheriff" in the park; he or she is also the medic, fireman, rescuer, teacher, game warden, and biologist. Larry knew I had a lot more to learn.

In August he sent me to Santa Fe, New Mexico, for search and rescue training. Over the summer I had also received training in wildland fire fighting, boating and advanced law enforcement subjects. During the fall and winter I attended classes in safety, supervision, and more law enforcement; in December I attended the Orientation to the National Park Service course at the Albright Training Center on the South Rim of the Grand Canyon. Since that class was intended for entry level employees I didn't learn anything new, but I thoroughly enjoyed my stay at Grand Canyon. In the spring I went to Chickasaw National Recreation Area for more SCUBA classes, and then it was back to Meredith for underwater search and sonar training. By the time my second summer at Meredith rolled around I was much better prepared.

During the winter of 1985-86 when I wasn't attending classes, I occupied myself with various projects. One of these projects was upgrading the lake's navigational aids. This job actually belonged to Barney, the boat mechanic and navigation aid technician. Barney appreciated my help and we became good friends. Because he allowed me to work in his shop, I was able to completely overhaul each of our patrol boats. I painted, installed new equipment and refinished the wood on the boats. Chief Larry once told me to make sure our boats always looked good if they happened to be on TV. I don't know about the Chief, but I was proud whenever our patrol boats appeared on the evening news.

I enjoyed my work, but home life was as lonely as it had been the winter before. Eileen was in her second year of law school. We couldn't afford to visit on the telephone, so I sent her letters every week. Not surprisingly, when winter arrived in Minnesota, Eileen's letters reported how cold it was and told about the deep snow. I felt compelled to defend Texas; because of course everything is bigger or in this case, deeper, in Texas. Since often on cold, mid-winter days there wasn't a single visitor in the park, I had plenty of time to defend Texas's honor and do something to amuse Eileen. After a three-inch snowstorm I spent an entire shift scraping and piling up the white stuff in front of the ranger station. When the pile was big enough I got behind it and had my picture taken.

It did, in fact, get very cold in the Texas Panhandle. That winter we had several good snowstorms and the lake froze over. One of my early morning duties during the coldest days was to go to the marina, clear the snow off of the boats, and break up the ice around the hulls that threatened to freeze the boats into their slips. We were in essence the Coast Guard of Lake Meredith and we had to be ready for rescues day or night, winter or summer.

One cold winter evening I was called to assist John in a search and rescue mission. That night I learned a valuable lesson. Boating classes are great, but experience reinforces lessons and makes them unforgettable.

John called me at home to say that two fishermen had not returned. I met him at the station and together we drove to the boat slips. Because a light breeze made the night feel even colder than the actual temperature, we chose the *Revenge*, our larger, heavy-weather boat for this mission. The *Revenge* had two engines, a semi-enclosed cockpit when the weather curtains were rigged in place and a small but comfortable cabin below deck and forward of the cockpit.

106

John knew the area of the lake frequented by fishermen and we were soon paralleling that dark, rocky shoreline. As I played the search light back and forth across the beaches, I heard John call out, "There they are!"

The fishermen had known the Park Service would be along sooner or later to pick them up and had built a fire both for warmth and as a signal. The wind, which had been light when we left the slips, was now a stiff breeze blowing onto the land. Because of the danger posed by the rocky shore and the direction of the wind we looked the situation over from a safe distance.

In the bright glare of the searchlight we saw a small boat squatting half in and half out of the water. Mashed down into the sand, the boat was apparently full of water and the stern rocked slowly in the breaking waves. Two big men stood nearby. It was hard to tell how big they were but, even at that distance, it looked as if the two of them had pushed the carrying capacity of their small boat.

John maneuvered us to within a couple hundred feet of the beach. Motoring into the beach was out of the question. Ideally, John would have dropped me off on the beach to look the situation over and make the tow hookup, but the combination of wind and rocky shoreline made that impossible. John and I discussed having the men walk down the beach to a spot where we could safely get in to pick them up. But rescuing the men and leaving their boat didn't seem right.

It had long been the philosophy of the Lake District that providing service was as important as performing law enforcement. John always said, "Service is our last name," and our commitment to service was proudly proclaimed in big gold letters on the dock where we moored our boats. That sign said, "To Protect and Serve."

Since the men looked fit and able to assist in their own rescue and the boat, while clearly swamped, looked sound and towable we decided to save both the men and their boat. Using our public address system, John related our plan to the fishermen. They signaled back with thumbs up and began bailing the water out of their boat. While they were getting ready, John maneuvered as close to shore as he dared. He continuously worked the helm and throttles to hold us stationary against the breakers. When in position, I cast out the tow line and it was blown ashore. One of the men waded out, recovered the end of the tow line and snapped it onto their boat's bow eye. Still using the public address system, John instructed the men to put on their life jackets. When all was ready and the fishermen had climbed into their small boat, I turned and called out to John, "They're ready, let's go."

John eased the throttles forward and the last loops of slack slowly played out, the line rose out of the water and became taut. The deck under me vibrated with the power of our twin engines but the little fishing boat did not move.

Our engines roared and foamy white water boiled up around our stern. The tow line stretched and groaned. Suddenly I realized the line could break and snap back. Expecting this whiplash, I stepped back. For twenty seconds the tug-of-war continued. Then slowly the little boat began to slide backwards off the beach before pivoting and falling in line behind us.

Immediately I noticed the small boat's bow was too high, as if some great weight was pushing down its stern. I couldn't see our fishermen because of the rakish angle. I yelled, "Something's wrong!"

Upon hearing my warning, John instinctively pulled back on the throttles. The moment the power slackened, the little boat reared backwards. Its bow rose up, or more precisely its stern sank down, until the small vessel was nearly vertical. It hung there for a moment and then slowly glided backwards and silently slipped beneath the waves. It seemed like slow motion to me, yet in reality the swiftness of the disaster had precluded any action on our part.

I was still staring at the spot where the boat had disappeared when John's excited voice galvanized me into action, "The towline! Cut the towline!" The weight of the diving boat was pulling us backwards. The line angled down steeper and steeper into the black water and the tow line was stretched tight under its load. I couldn't unhook it. I fumbled for my knife, cursed my slowness and finally with a quick sawing action cut the line.

With the release of the line came a new horror. Where were the two fishermen? I couldn't remember seeing them after we left the beach.

I grabbed the hand-held searchlight and began panning the beam over the water. Only choppy waves were visible in the small circle of light. Back and forth I scanned. My panic rose with each passing second. John maneuvered the patrol boat back towards the accident site. He kept calling out, "Do you see them?"

I strained to see through the darkness. We were now engaged in a life or death task. Literally everything, their very next sunrise, the next hug from family, everything that was to ever happen to these two men now depended on our performance.

The patrol boat was almost directly over the spot where the boat had sunk before I caught my first glimpse of two heads bobbing in the water. They were less than two boat lengths away. John expertly pulled alongside the motionless forms. I stretched as far over the side as I could and caught each man by his life jacket. John joined me at the gunnel and together we attempted to pull the first man aboard. But these men were BIG and try as we might, we couldn't raise the man high enough to pull him aboard. Every second counted. We didn't have time to rig some elaborate method to hoist them out of the water. They were literally slowly dying. Although dangerous in these kinds of seas, this close to shore, John made a snap decision to kill our engines and board the men over the stern. It was the lowest point on our boat's hull.

With both of us straining, we dragged each man between the out-drives and onto the deck. It was a brutal, ungraceful method and in any other situation we would have received complaints for being so rough. Even though the two had only been in the water for a few minutes, they were hypothermic. We radioed for an ambulance to meet us at Fritch Fortress launch ramp and set out as fast as we could in the rough seas.

The two fishermen didn't hold the mishap against us, but John and I both felt bad about it. To make amends we later dove on their boat and helped them recover it from about sixty feet of water. The whole affair served up some important lessons for me. The most important of which was, I still had a lot to learn.

- 16 -

Summer of Hard Knocks

The summer of 1986 began with a bang. On second thought, it was actually more of a screech, thump, thump—the unmistakable sound of a vehicle skidding off the road and rolling over.

This was the first significant event of the season—an auto accident. I stepped out the front door of the ranger station and heard the screech, thump, thump and saw a cloud of dust less than a hundred yards away. Immediately I popped my head back inside and yelled, "We've got a wreck!"

After alerting the staff in the ranger station, I jumped into my truck and drove the short distance to the park entrance road where a pickup truck lay on its side at the base of an embankment. Its wheels, facing the highway, were still spinning. Debris was scattered about, but I couldn't see anyone. I parked a short distance past the accident, grabbed my EMT medical bag and I jumped out.

At the same time Bob Wilson pulled up, stopped just above the wreck, bailed out, and ran down the slope. A few steps ahead of me, Bob disappeared behind the truck and then a second later reappeared running back up the bank. As we passed each other he yelled, "I got traffic control!"

I didn't know what Bob had seen, but I thought if an experienced ranger like Bob runs away from the scene, it's got to be bad. I rounded the truck and—it was bad. On the ground, a man was sticking out from under the cab, facedown. The truck lay across him and only his upper back, arms and head were uncovered. His skin was dark from all the blood being squeezed into his upper torso and the weight of the vehicle was crushing him. He was unconscious and his breathing was labored. Standing next to him was a second man. His face was scuffed and one arm from above the elbow was missing. All I could see was an empty shirt sleeve.

I had to decide who I should treat first, who I could most help. The man under the truck was going to die and there was nothing I could do at that moment to help him. I couldn't turn him or even open his airway. Nothing would change his fate unless the truck was lifted.

The man without an arm was also at risk, he could bleed to death. I could do something about that. I grabbed a surgical dressing and pushed it up the empty sleeve onto the stump. He looked puzzled and then said, "No man, it's been gone for years!"

Since that fellow was in no danger of bleeding to death, I turned back to the man under the truck. Later I would laugh at my attempt to save a one-armed man, but at that moment all my attention was on the second victim. Suddenly, Nancy and Rod appeared and knowing we had to move the truck I sent them to the maintenance shop to get jacks and cribbing. They took off and I turned back to the man under the truck. I attempted to get an oxygen mask over his face even though I knew the situation was hopeless. The man was going to stop breathing at any moment.

Just then, Bob and six men raced around the end of the truck. Bob had stopped all traffic and recruited every able-bodied man. He ordered these men to grab the truck and lift. My first instinct was that this was not a good plan. What if they dropped the truck or it rolled over on the man's head? But one glance at the victim now turning dark purple and giving his last few gasps told me we couldn't wait. I instructed this team to get a good grip and lift on my count of three. I positioned myself at the victim's head, my hands under his arms, ready to pull him free if the plan worked. The men lifted. The truck moved and I pulled. The man slid out.

Once he was free, we log-rolled him over and he immediately began breathing. The Fritch volunteer ambulance arrived and the crew took over. As it turned out, the man who was minutes from dying,

Picnic at Toroweap Overlook on the Grand Canyon. **From left to right:** *Chuck, Grandma Craig, Ranger John Riffey, Brother Dave, Cousin Sharon, Cousin Carol, Riffey's nephew Johnny.*

Craig Ranch – Chuck with saddle and bridle stands in front of the barn's saddle shop.

Lake Meredith National Recreation Area, 1986 – Sentry patrol boat.

Lake Meredith National Recreation Area, 1986 - 87 – Aboard patrol boat Revenge.

Right: Getting ready to dive. Putting on dry suit. Does not look happy.

Below: Search and Rescue Training.

Lake Mead tunnel fire, 1990.

Grand Canyon North Rim – Hand crew on Wildland fire assignment. Chuck is in the front row, far right.

Lake Mead National Recreation Area – Spike Cody and Jim Sanborn rest beside the Rim Trail.

Search and Rescue – Shivwits reconnaissance trip.

Hunting patrol at Shivwits, 1993.

Captain of Engine 4.

Top left: *Willow Beach District Ranger Bill Sherman;* **Top right:** *Boulder Beach District Ranger Bob McKeever;* **Above:** *Lake Meredith National Recreation Area, 1986 – Ranger Bob Wilson befriends a small visitor.*

Above: Chuck and Eileen –
Two very different people,
two very different careers,
one happily married couple.

Left: Eileen O'Neill, 1980 –
Ready to climb Lodge Rock
at Lake Mead National
Recreation Area.

not only lived, but had only minor injuries. All his rescuers received a commendation from the Regional Director.

Saving a man's life was a tremendous boost to my ego and I was also beginning to feel confident about my boating skills. In fact I was overconfident, because I still had a lot to learn about the hazards of heavy weather. But I was anxious to start saving lives on the water and that's when Mother Nature taught me a lesson.

The monsoon began in late July. Each afternoon somewhere on the horizon, towering cauliflower-like cumulonimbus clouds welled up. These massively powerful clouds with their magnificent lightning shows were beautiful. To me they also represented excitement, a chance to perform rescues and save inexperienced boaters on Lake Meredith's high seas. Such ideas were melodramatic, but my romantic view of rangering colored any serious thoughts on the matter. The fact that such storms could be dangerous to me never crossed my mind.

On the night I learned my lesson, the phone rang minutes after I arrived home. I was pulling off my boots when I picked up the phone and listened as the Chief explained that the Weather Service had called with the report of a big thunderstorm over Dumas that was moving our way. Larry directed me to take a boat out and warn boaters and beach campers. I put my boots back on, apologized to Eileen for missing yet another dinner, and rushed out the door trying to hide my joyful anticipation from her. This was a night for heroes and I wanted to be in the thick of it.

It was completely dark by the time I arrived at the ranger station, yet every few seconds the scene was illuminated by flashes of lightning—a sure sign of a rapidly approaching storm. Nancy was waiting beside our patrol truck, her gear already loaded. I loaded mine quickly and we headed for the marina. On the way, I talked nonstop about the storm and what we were going to do. Nancy, younger, yet in this instance wiser than me, was quiet.

At the slips I opted for the *Whaler*. It was a seaworthy craft and I didn't feel any trepidation about taking her out into the storm that was closing in. The water of the harbor remained calm and lights from the marina danced on its surface, but the thunder was no longer a distant rumble and each flash of lightning was followed by a loud "Ka-bang!"

We started motoring down the north shore, stopping each time we came to a beach camp to issue warnings and advice. This was my kind of rangering. I'd had more than enough of dealing with law enforcement and people problems. I saw myself as a different kind of ranger, the consummate good guy, not unlike my role model John Riffey. Rescue work was not only the ultimate good guy activity; it was also adrenaline-pumping fun.

Initially it had been our intent to tell everyone to get off the lake, but now it was too late to run. Instead, we instructed beach campers to batten the hatches and prepare for high winds. I should have listened to my own advice.

A breeze was building and the lake's turbulent surface swallowed all light, making the night darker except for the rapid fire lightning flashes. Cautiously we felt our way up the lake. Each time lightning flashed I could make out the silhouette of the shoreline a few hundred feet to starboard. I was thinking about how heroes were made, while Nancy, on the other hand, was very quiet—probably thinking about how fools like us could get in trouble.

As we eased up the narrow channel between the shore and Arrowhead Island I heard the drumming rain and roaring wind bearing down upon us. One moment we were in a stiff breeze, the next a gale. It was like an avalanche of wind and rain rolled onto us. The patrol boat heeled over. The rain came like bullets on a flat trajectory, beating on the windscreen and slapping our faces. I ducked down behind the glass and yelled to Nancy to break out the rain gear and the weather curtains. I don't think she heard my words, but she could see what was needed, knew what to do and disappeared below.

Nancy emerged a minute later with her yellow raincoat on and holding the weather curtains. Together we tried to fasten the curtains in place. Each time we tried the wind ripped them away. Water washed over the deck and all my thoughts of being a hero were replaced by fear. I didn't know how close we were to the rocky shoreline of Arrowhead

Island or any number of rocky reefs in the area. Were we motoring towards open water or a disastrous grounding? I had no idea.

"Get the searchlight," I yelled. Nancy switched on the light and instantly things went from bad to worse. The powerful beam lit up little more than a few feet beyond our bow. All I could see was a sheet of rain. "Turn it off," I yelled, but it was already too late. My night vision was wrecked; and the boat, it seemed, would soon suffer the same fate.

I reached for the radio. Maybe one of the Sanford-Yake night shift rangers could help. Bob Wilson answered. He could tell by the panic in my voice that I was in trouble. He said he would go to Fitch Fortress, turn on all his lights and hope that I would be able to see them to give me a reference point. But with the rain whipping horizontally over the windscreen and striking my face, I knew there was no way I would be able to see his lights. Nevertheless, I squinted—forced myself to look into the driving rain, but all I saw were sheets of rain and absolute blackness.

What could I do? I could keep going the way I was headed and take my chances. Sooner or later I would arrive at a shoreline. But would I see land before I ran aground? I could turn around and go back, but what was behind us? Or maybe I could stay put. This seemed the best option.

I throttled back and allowed the boat to just barely maintain steerage. Still, without any outside reference point I did not know if we were slowly creeping forward or falling back. At any moment I expected jagged rocks, like sharks' teeth, to rise up out of the sea and crush my small craft.

It seemed like an eternity, but in reality was more like half an hour. Then, almost as abruptly as it had begun, it ended. The rain stopped. The wind calmed to a gentle breeze. I relaxed my grip on the helm and looked around. The patrol boat was a mess. Everything had been tossed about and everything was soaked, including our radio. The speaker now gurgled and there were a couple of inches of water on the cabin deck. However, the most severely damaged item was my spirit. During the storm we had been in no position to help anyone and in fact we almost needed rescue ourselves. Fortunately, no one had called for our assistance.

That day I learned I wasn't the hotshot skipper I had thought I was and I learned to have respect for Mother Nature. But I had more to learn that summer. My next lesson would superficially seem to be about the unfairness of the world. What it was really about was the courage to do the right thing, even when you pay a personal price.

Fritch, Texas, was a small community—widely spread out and sharing a common boundary with Lake Meredith. Because our headquarters were in Fritch, several staff members, including the Chief Ranger, were members of its volunteer fire department.

One afternoon, a fire started among the houses spread out across the grassy prairie adjacent to the park boundary. The fire, pushed by a steady breeze, began to outrun and overwhelm the volunteer fire crews. In a panic, the Fritch Fire Chief called Lake Meredith and asked for help.

The dispatcher receiving the call began a frantic search for the proper authority to take the call. But the Superintendent and Chief of Maintenance had gone to the far end of the park and were out of radio contact and the Chief Ranger was already at the fire as a volunteer. No one knew where the Park Administrative Officer was and there were no District Rangers on duty.

As I was driving to work, I saw the smoke coming from somewhere outside the park. In fact, the fire was clearly visible from the ranger station, but I figured the Fritch Fire Department had it under control until I received a radio message to call the dispatcher on the phone right away. When I called, the dispatcher said Fritch Fire Department was asking for help. She told me that the Superintendent and the Chief of Maintenance were out of radio contact at the far end of the lake and she couldn't locate anyone in authority. Suddenly I realized that I, a lowly GS-5, was the most authority she could find.

The decision wasn't even difficult. All my life I had been raised to do the right thing. Fritch needed help. They were asking for help and I would send help. Without hesitation I took charge. I instructed the dispatcher to have the maintenance crew and seasonal rangers meet me at the fire cache. The dispatcher immediately began putting out the calls.

At the cache we quickly hitched up the two trailer pumpers and loaded the trucks with tools. As people reported in, I assigned them to one of the units and sent them on their way. When finished, I followed the last pumper to the fire.

By the time we arrived, the fire had burned ten acres and was threatening a number of houses. The Fritch Fire Chief instructed us to defend as many houses as possible. Even though we were in front of the advancing fire, which is normally a big "no-no" we had the street as a safety zone and we were able to stand our ground.

We fought each run of the fire as it came up and at the end of the fight, only one house was lost. The park crews had clearly saved two and I was proud of our effort. Therefore, I never saw it coming, when I was told I was to be officially reprimanded.

The next day I was called to headquarters and the Chief told me that I had acted without authority. So who had the authority? The Administrative Officer. She had been in her office with the door closed eating her lunch and no one knew she was there. However, when she came out and discovered what was going on she was, as the saying goes, "mad as a wet hen."

The reprimand was bad enough, but when I was told that all personnel on the fire would be put on leave without pay for the duration of the fire, it was more than I could take. I said I would accept the leave without pay, but I protested the injustice of punishing people who were acting on my orders. I also pointed out to the Chief that he had been at the fire. He and I had talked briefly and he hadn't said anything about my acting without authority. Larry seemed to consider this, but still waved me out of his office. I returned to the ranger station mad as hell.

I never received the reprimand and I never asked why not. I can only speculate that Larry had a change of heart or the Superintendent changed it for him. No one was docked pay and in fact I don't think any of the others ever knew their pay was at risk. But I didn't forget. The incident hardened my heart towards those I considered bureaucrats.

Never again would I be surprised by the rigidness of bureaucracy or the vindictiveness of a hurt ego.

All I can say is I did the right thing and I would do it again.

- 17 -

Pushing Hard

Looking back at my performance appraisals, I see a change in my attitude beginning in the winter of '86-'87. I call it hard charging. My boss called it "easily frustrated" and "insensitive." Good enough wasn't good enough for me. After my summer of hard knocks, I toughened up, worked harder and, as my appraisals reflected, pushed harder.

In the fall I registered for an Emergency Medical Technician (EMT) class. I also enrolled in management and supervision classes at Frank Phillip's Community College and I began working with weights at the college gym.

In late October after Eileen returned to school, Larry sent me on my first big wildland fire assignment. I had trained and been certified as a firefighter during the summer and I had been chomping at the bit to be assigned to a hand crew, but I had asked Larry to hold off on sending me out until Eileen left.

The fire season should have been over, but a dry season had hampered all attempts to put out the Deadwood fire in Idaho. Crews had been fighting for a month. Fresh troops were needed and Larry sent me.

I was flown by small plane to the Forest Service mobilization center in Albuquerque, New Mexico. There I was assigned to a crew and put on a plane to Boise. In Boise my crew boarded a tired, old school bus and we traveled north to the fire.

Many on the crew were old hands, so I watched and did what they did. Even, so I'm sure my inexperience was obvious. Fortunately,

119

an old salt took me under his wing and offered advice and instruction. He pointed out that my gear was woefully lacking, helped me secure a new fire pack and directed me to the base camp commissary for boots and long johns. He said it was going to be cold at night and he was right. Before I left that fire, it snowed on us.

The nights were cold and the days were brutal. Twelve- to sixteen- hour shifts of continuous chopping and digging in the dusty, dry earth was not how I had imagined fire fighting. It was more like being on a chain gang and I rarely saw any fire. What I did see were blackened trees and earth where the fire had already come and gone. On one day, however, we were moved in close to the fire. The fire, still hundreds of yards away, puffed and belched as it crept through the foot-thick duff and every once in a while, as if to warn us it was still dangerous, it would engulf a tree in a matter of seconds. Eighty-foot conifers would be consumed in a frightening roar. Each time a tree went up I looked to the others on the crew for any signs of concern, but their backs stayed bent and they continued digging.

After two weeks it snowed and the wet snow cooled and smothered the flames. Nature did what man could not.

On the flight back to Albuquerque I started to feel sick. By the time we were back at the mobilization center I was really sick. For the next twenty-some hours I lay on a cot waiting for my number to be called and wishing I could die. Finally my travel orders came through. Back home the doc told me I had one of the finest cases of strep throat he had ever seen.

I have since learned that my illness was not unusual. The long hours and harsh working conditions, plus close contact with others, made fire crews on the Deadwood fire susceptible to contagious diseases.

With all my training and fire fighting experience, I began to think of myself as a fully qualified ranger. In retrospect I realize I had become a "know-it-all." I was like a teenager who believes he knows more than his parents. With Eileen away at school, I spent most of my time at work and became impatient with my superiors and Park Service red tape. When I saw something that needed to be done, I did it. This resulted in some mistakes.

For instance, I noticed that cars were being parked in a haphazard way at the ranger station. What we needed, I decided, were marked spaces. I carefully measured and painted lines. If I had stopped at that, everything would have been fine. But I decided to assign each space to an employee. Starting with the lowest number and continuing on to the highest number, I painted every employee's radio call number on a space. This resulted in some newcomers getting prime parking and some with seniority finding their spot at the far end of the lot. Big mistake! The next day I was out in the parking lot carefully painting over the call numbers.

Another mistake was the day I decided to burn the tall, dead grass in the buoy storage area. I won't go into the details but I didn't just burn up the grass; I also burned the used buoys hanging in racks and the new buoys still in their packing crates.

Other times, my problems came from being overcommitted. Because a missing person often turns up as a floating body, my boss and I were patrolling the lake twice a day. On the third day, heavy weather made this task dangerous and my boss told me that we wouldn't go out. This seemed to me to be neglect of duty, so I went out on my own. I didn't find a floater, but I did get told about the importance of following orders.

Later that winter I became quite angry at a slow, bumbling response to a missing person report, which resulted in our finding a body instead of a person. When a hunter didn't return home one evening his wife called the police and was told no action would be taken for twenty-four hours. I'm certain if the wife had called the Park Service we would have begun a search immediately. However, when the search began, what should have been a simple matter of following tracks in fresh snow from the parked vehicle to the lost hunter was compromised by too many searchers using ineffective search techniques. I chafed under this bureaucratic response that resulted in a loss of life.

Even though I was becoming very serious about rangering, even though I was sure I knew more about the job than my superiors,

121

I still had a sense of humor and time for practical jokes. So when the Chief Ranger went on vacation and the number two ranger, Duane, was made acting chief during Larry's absence, a co-worker, Pete, and I had some fun redecorating the Chief's office. On the eve before Larry was to return we sneaked into his office and piled his personal things in a corner and then decorated the room to look as if Duane had taken over. We removed the Chief's name plate on his desk and replaced it with Duane's. We even went so far as to replace Larry's family pictures.

Larry found the prank amusing. Unfortunately the Administrative Officer, who had wanted to hang me for the Fritch fire, wasn't at all amused. She wanted me reprimanded again.

Then along came a-once-in-a-lifetime opportunity to have some fun. One day a group of us in the ranger station overheard a rough, noisy maintenance operator use some coarse language to describe a backcountry pit toilet on the radio. This was prohibited by policy. All of us in the ranger station who heard the transmission laughed and someone in the group mentioned that this fellow had better re-read the radio manual.

Suddenly I had an idea. That evening, after everyone had left the office, I copied a page out of the radio manual and highlighted the section prohibiting profanity. I placed the page in an official interoffice routing envelope and addressed it to the offending operator. On my way home I dropped it in the park mail basket.

The following morning the operator burst into the ranger station waving the highlighted page. He yelled, "Look what headquarters sent me." The page was passed around and there was plenty of false concern expressed and a few discreet winks. When the offending paper reached me I said, "Better be careful! Someone at the HQ is watching you."

His response had been better than anything I could have hoped for. So a few days later I copied another page out of the disciplinary action manual. I picked a violation I knew the man was good for and highlighted it. Again I mailed it to him through official channels. The next day he stormed around showing every ranger and maintenance man the paper, all the while ranting and raving about the S.O.B.s at headquarters.

This was so good I couldn't stop. Once a week for the next several weeks I copied a page from the discipline manual and sent it to him. I was always careful to type the address using someone else's typewriter and mailed the pages on different days and at different times. With each new page the operator issued more threats.

Finally, the operator took his latest page and stormed into headquarters. Naturally the Chief of Maintenance had no idea what he was so upset about and assured him that no one at Headquarters was reprimanding him. The operator's next stop was the Superintendent's office where he demanded that the perpetrator of this terrible defamation be caught and severely punished. Vicky, one of the headquarters office staff, overheard the loud discussion. She was one of the few who knew I was the perpetrator and she called me at home. She warned me to be careful. However, I wasn't worried. I had been too tricky.

But after lunch I received a radio message that the Superintendent wanted to see me. A flash of panic hit me. I thought, "He knows."

I pulled into the headquarters parking lot with suppressed trepidation. It was no longer suppressed as soon as I stepped through the front door. Superintendent John was standing in the lobby waiting for me. "I want to see you in my office," he said without smiling. I thought, "Oh no, he knows. How, I don't know, but he knows." I followed the old man back like a prisoner going to the gallows.

John had over forty years of service and in his younger days it was said that he was a hard charger. Now he was pretty mellow, but still he was not a man to trifle with. He pushed a pile of papers out of his way onto the floor, moved behind his desk and sat down. I took the obligatory position of the condemned at attention in front of the desk. Sweat was already beading on my brow.

He told me to sit down, looked for something in the clutter on his desk, found it and said, "I'd like you to look at this."

Suddenly I knew I wasn't about to be suspended or worse. My relief was overwhelming. I couldn't listen. I couldn't talk. I sat in shocked silence. After a few seconds he asked, "Are you okay?"

When I found my voice I said, "Sir, I thought you wanted to see me for something else." And then I confessed.

The Superintendent cut me off with a wave of his hand. He leaned back slowly in his chair. The silence was crushing. Then he smiled and said, "Keep up the good work, son." That was it. John had his critics, but in my mind at that moment I saw the real ranger and leader.

The winter of '86-'87 was the beginning of my pushing hard period. It would last until I once again became a District Ranger. During this period of my career I wanted to know it all and do it all. Fortunately for me, Lake Meredith was a busy place with a small staff. As a result there were lots of opportunities. Anything that I was interested in, I could usually get involved in. Want to work on a special project, just volunteer. Want to be part of an incident response, simply show up. Law enforcement, search and rescue, fire fighting—you didn't have to know anything; you merely had to show initiative and the very next thing you knew you were in the game.

I worked hard, but I was often impatient and frustrated with the bureaucracy. I believe my impatience irritated my superiors at times. Later I would learn not to buck the system. Eventually I would learn the secret to a successful life is being able to blend dreams with reality.

- 18 -

The NPS Navy

I thought of the Lake District as the NPS Navy. It was an easy reach to think that way, given the military nature of the park organization and, in my mind, we were professional sailors. I felt we were the guardians of all those who ventured upon our little "ocean." Of course this was a romantic, even dramatic, way of thinking.

I also had an elitist attitude. This stemmed from the fact that the lake was the whole point of the place. The lake was why people came to the park. My attitude also came from the way Larry treated us. The Lake District vied with the Sanford-Yake District for his attention and park money. Because maintaining and operating boats is expensive, the Lake District got the lion's share of the ranger division budget. I'm sure the other districts' rangers were envious.

Now this elitist attitude can either be very good or very bad. If you can back up your claim, if you can walk the walk and not just talk the talk, you will have the respect of your peers and appreciation of the organization. However, if you can't, you will be the object of scorn. Therefore I made sure I could back up any claims of superiority.

I worked hard to improve my boating skills and knowledge. My growth had started slowly, but over time had accelerated. By 1987 my boating skills had become finely honed.

At the same time I was coming into my own, the Lake District was also changing, growing and becoming professional. John and I both worked on our training programs, developing new courses and standards. We also updated, improved, and replaced our equipment and vessels. Our efforts were bolstered by the good fortune of hiring

125

two excellent seasonal rangers. Nancy had moved on to Yellowstone and in her place were Rod, a college student, and Mike, a school teacher. All of these things came together that year to create as sharp, disciplined, and professional a work unit as could ever be hoped for. We were the "NPS Navy."

The purpose of our little navy, ultimately, was to save lives. There is no telling how many lives we saved indirectly by our constant preaching about wearing life jackets, inspecting visitors' boats, or warning them of approaching storms. But we directly chalked up a number of saves and it was those saves that made it all worthwhile.

One of those saves occurred on an evening when I was patrolling Blue West. I noticed a small ski boat adrift. On board were some half dozen, loud, and boisterous young men. I was still several hundred yards away when one of the men jumped overboard and swam away. About twenty yards from the boat he ran out of steam. As I watched, his play turned into distress. He called out for help and started thrashing his arms down into the water. It was the last panicky throes of a drowning man.

I jammed the throttles down and raced forward. Cutting the power at just the right moment, I glided up beside him and dropped a ring buoy into his arms. His certain death was cancelled that day. After I dragged him aboard I learned that he and his friends were celebrating his last day as a bachelor. They were all intoxicated and he thought it would be funny to take the keys to the boat and go for a swim.

On that day I saved a life, but sadly, there were other times when our presence made no difference at all. On a very windy day when no one with good sense should have been out, my deckhand spotted a boat in open water off of Cedar Canyon. It wasn't moving and we suspected it was disabled and adrift. Why else would a boat be dead in the water in the middle of the lake on such a windy day?

But as we motored closer we saw that there was a man in the water attempting to water ski. I thought, "You've gotta be kidding!" It was unbelievable, but not illegal. When we came close enough I shouted advice, suggesting that they seek shelter. The operator seemed to agree, but said they were going to try "just one more time."

126

As we pulled away, still watching, we saw them try to pull the skier up—he fell. Instead of helping the skier back into the boat, they circled around to try again. Since they had not heeded our advice and apparently were not going to, we motored away.

Later, we learned that shortly after we left, the skier got in trouble. The three people on board moved to the same side of the boat and it capsized. One person disappeared and the others clung to the hull and floated across the lake. Sometime after dark, one of them hiked to a nearby community and called for help.

Called back into service, I spent the night running search patterns looking for the missing man. I spent the next few weeks looking for his body.

While it may have been a stretch to think of ourselves as a navy, it was by no means an exaggeration to be compared to the Coast Guard. And like the Coast Guard, storms were the source of much of our business and the many opportunities to do what we did best—help people.

For instance, one cold and windy fall day I came to the aid of an elderly gentleman who was devastated by the loss of his forty-two-foot houseboat. When I arrived on the scene it was too late to save his boat, but I did what I could to comfort and help him.

The man's big mistake had been taking the boat out on a windy day when large waves were breaking over the bow. There were two forward-facing windows at deck level on this boat. The waves crashing on board broke out the windows and then with each successive wave water poured into the forward compartment. Fearing that he was about to sink, the old man purposely ran the boat aground on the closest shore. Unfortunately his chosen spot was very rocky and fully exposed to the breaking surf. The houseboat was quickly holed by sharp rocks and settled down with a sharp list to starboard. I received the mayday call not long after that.

When I arrived at the accident site, the old man was safely on shore, but it was already apparent that his boat was going to be a total loss. Waves were surging over the deck and the sharply tilted craft had four to five feet of water in the main cabin. The pounding surf was slowly breaking the vessel apart and flinging the pieces onto the rocks.

The old man sat staring at his dying boat. We talked for several minutes and then he asked if I could get some things off the boat for him. I studied the listing craft for a long minute. Boarding the now partly submerged vessel was clearly not a smart thing to do, but I reasoned I could be in and out quickly. Because I knew retrieving his prize possessions would make a difference in the old man's life, I agreed to try.

I took off my leather duty-belt, revolver and radio. I left them with the old man and cautiously climbed up the hull, over the rail and onto the deck. Each time a wave crashed into the seaward side of the boat, it shook and rivers of water surged into the cabin. I peered into the dark interior, watching the water rise and fall in rhythmic fashion. Glancing back at the old man, who was watching me intently, I decided to go inside. I stepped down into the flooded cabin. The cold water came up to my knees, but the further I ventured in, the deeper the water became. I began quickly gathering the requested items and anything else I could easily carry. As I worked, I noticed the starboard side of the cabin visibly deflected inward with each slam of a wave.

The wallet and car keys, the main objectives of my mission, were forward near the helm. I crossed the cabin to reach them. Everything was where the old man said it would be. As I stuffed everything into a coat pocket and turned to retreat, there was a loud crack. The side of the cabin pushed inward. A gap appeared between the bulkhead and overhead. It was time to get out.

Back on land, soaking wet and cold, I handed the few recovered items to the old man. His eyes were damp with emotion and I could see how grateful he was. Monday morning quarterbacks would probably say it was foolish to board a flooded houseboat just to recover property. But I knew the risks and judged that what I did was worth it.

My memories of that 1987 summer and the "NPS Navy" make me proud of my accomplishments. This was a high point of my ranger career.

- 19 -

Crazy Times

My third summer at Lake Meredith was punctuated by several events that could be described as crazy, or if not crazy, certainly unexpected and interesting. Summer began normal enough. It was the same old routine for us in boats, but routine came to an end with the arrival of the monsoon in July.

One hot and steamy evening, Eileen and I drove into Amarillo to meet my mom and dad. They were passing through on their way home after visiting in Oklahoma and we met for dinner. While we were eating, thunderstorms banged away all around. When we got ready to head home, a particularly dark and nasty storm was lingering to the north in the vicinity of Borger. I gave it little thought until we got closer to Borger and it became more evident that a very severe storm had passed through. When we were within a few blocks of our apartment we saw trees and tree limbs in the road and when we rounded the last turn we saw flashing red lights, police cars and fire engines. A policeman stopped us saying a tornado had struck the Fairlanes Apartments. That was where we lived. At first he wasn't going to let me pass, but finally he agreed to let me go. We owned next to nothing and if it had all gone to Oz it wouldn't have mattered much. But I was worried about our cat in the apartment.

From the outside our second floor apartment didn't look too bad. The porch roof was missing, but I couldn't see any other damage. However, when I opened the door an amazing sight greeted me. There was no roof, no ceiling, nothing above the top of the walls. All else seemed undisturbed and our cat was sitting in the center of the room patiently waiting for me.

After rescuing Kit Carson, I switched to the problem of salvaging our few belongings. I turned to Larry, the only person I could think of for help, and within half an hour he and a number of the other rangers were on my doorstep. In a steady rain, my co-workers moved everything I owned to a nearby empty apartment. Their effort in the middle of the night was a true act of friendship.

The next crazy event that summer was the silliness known as the Harmonic Convergence. In August I was sent to Chaco Canyon, New Mexico, to assist the local staff with the management of this event. I don't even pretend to understand it, but apparently, the Harmonic Convergence was a sort of New Age, world-changing event based on the Mayan calendar. Groups of believers gathered at a number of sacred places around the world to pray and conduct ceremonies. Chaco Canyon, a Park Service site, was one of the sacred places.

Chaco Culture National Historic Park is a small, isolated park with limited facilities and resources. It was created to protect the numerous fragile and beautiful Anazazi ruins. Dozens of stone pueblos and kivas dot the canyon floor and the harmonic crowd had asked for and received permission to hold their ceremonies in a few of these places. While the Park Service felt obligated to treat the gathering as a mainstream event, it had serious concerns about protecting the cultural resources. As a measure to protect the park, the Southwest Regional Special Events Team, or SET, was brought in. SET was a team of about twenty handpicked rangers from all over the region. These rangers were sent to any park in the region whenever extra manpower was needed to manage an event.

I was not part of SET. It was an exclusive club for which you basically had to know somebody in order to get an invitation to join. My boss, John, however, was a member. When the call came for the SET to go to Chaco, John was able to select me as a substitute for a missing team member. They needed everybody for this one, so I was sent out of desperation.

At Chaco each morning after breakfast, we reported to an outdoor briefing area where we were given the latest "tactical" information and our assignments for the day. The group was broken down into two-person teams and dispatched to various sites around the canyon. Every two hours the teams would rotate to a new area just to break up the monotony, although I must say this was anything but boring. Entertaining would better describe the duty. The job we were to do was simple—be the friendly ranger and make sure everybody followed the park rules and did no harm to the ruins.

From my first moment in the field I knew this was not the usual crowd. The sounds of chanting, bongo drums, and humming crystal filled the air. There were hundreds of people walking around with feathers, quartz crystals, eagle talons, and even rabbits' feet. A few of the better-dressed had elaborate costumes complete with robes and staffs. Now from an infidel's perspective it seemed to me that everyone had a different take as to the purpose and meaning of the event. There were Indian wannabees, the astrology folks, the UFO people, New Age types, a few Mayan and Aztec followers, and dozens of other "spiritual" groups. Apparently the Harmonic Convergence had many meanings. It all depended on which religion, philosophy, or teaching the person happened to follow. It was all very confusing to try to understand and I must admit I didn't try very hard.

One of the sites I rotated to was a big kiva, Casa Rinconada. It is a large, circular, stone walled, well-like pit in the ground. The open-topped room can easily hold a hundred people. The park had given permission for ceremonies to be held in this chamber. People filed in and out of the kiva all day long to listen to a wide variety of sermons. I am not being insensitive, but some of the things I overheard while standing guard were, well, stupid. At one point, as I was looking down and listening to one particularly ridiculous speaker, two Navajos came up to the edge and peered over. They stood and listened for a time to some "Mother Earth, Father Sky" speech and then turned and walked away. As they left I heard one whisper, "Crazy white man."

A day later at our morning briefing, the park's Chief Ranger pointed to a butte across the valley and said, "That tower is a very sensitive archaeological site. No one is allowed to go up there." From the group someone said, "No one? How about that guy?" Sure enough, silhouetted against the sky at the top of Fajada Butte was a lone figure.

Two rangers were hastily dispatched to apprehend the trespasser. A short time later they radioed that they would need a patrol car to transport the violator. I happened to be standing around not looking busy enough, so I was sent out with a car.

The road did not go all the way to the base of the butte. I parked as close as I could and walked the half-mile over to meet with the other rangers and their captive. When we met, it was clear the rangers were either already tired of this case or were hoping to avoid the paperwork associated with an arrest, for they quickly turned the young man they were escorting over to me, instructed me to handle it, and promptly disappeared.

The trespasser seemed nice enough, completely non-threatening, polite, and cooperative. As we walked back to the road, I struck up a conversation. He told me about what he was doing and I explained why the NPS was concerned about the site. He knew he was being arrested; the other rangers had informed him of that, so when we reached the car he automatically stood by the back door.

"No, no," I said, "Get in the front." There are many law enforcement officers that would judge this to be a mistake. In my opinion however, if you're that uptight about everybody, if you can't judge character any better than that, maybe you shouldn't be in law enforcement. We chatted as I drove back to the command post.

There I had him take a seat while I determined what the park wanted done. Since the arresting officers had bailed out, it was decided that I should issue a citation and let the man go. While I agreed only a citation was warranted, I objected to being the one to do it. By rights, one of the other two rangers should have been the issuing officer. But they were hiding so I went ahead and issued the citation. The man accepted the ticket graciously and then I gave him a ride to his vehicle.

This would have all been an inconsequential event, forever forgotten by me, except several months later back at Lake Meredith, the Chief Ranger called me to his office and handed me a letter. He explained it had been sent to the Director of the National Park Service, the head honcho himself. It was a letter from the man I had ticketed at Chaco. He was a lawyer and student at Harvard Divinity School and his letter praised me for my kindness and professionalism.

Each day of the Harmonic Convergence was more fun than the one before. The last day was the best by far, made so by what happened on one of the roads into the park. Because the park's small campground couldn't even come close to holding all of the visitors, a temporary camping area had been set up outside the park. Shuttle buses ran down into Chaco Canyon and back to that camp. It was a perfect solution except for one small issue. Where the dirt road came off of the plateau and down into the canyon, it was only a single lane wide. In order to handle the heavy traffic on this short stretch of dugway, the park stationed a ranger at the top and bottom of the hill. Coordinating by radio they would let traffic run one way for a while and then the other. Up until the last day it had worked like a charm.

I was at the bottom when the fun began. An old truck towing a trailer with a water tank passed my station and started up at a slow, grinding pace. It was a hot, August day and the truck had been delivering drinking water to the masses. Now empty, it was on its way to get another load. I watched as the vehicle crawled up and then just above the half way point the driver tried to shift gears. The truck stalled. It then rolled backwards a few feet before stopping. But that few feet was all it took for the trailer to jack-knife across the road. Naturally it happened at the narrowest part of the dugway. The truck effectively blocked the road and would not start.

Looking at my watch, I knew the next shuttle bus was due at any moment. The ranger at the top walked down to see what was the problem. He reported that we needed a tow truck to clear the road. A call was made.

In the mean time, right on schedule, a bus pulled up. "It'll be just a few minutes," I told the driver. But a few minutes turned into half an hour and no progress was being made up on the hill. Soon I had several buses stacked up. It was hot in the sun and it was hotter inside the buses. Each time people started to get off I would say, "Please stay on the bus; it will only be a few more minutes." I knew that was a lie, but it was better to keep everyone bunched up out of the way than to have them wandering all over.

However, the tide was against me. I heard the rebel call, "Everybody, let's go. We'll pray for the truck to move." Out of the buses came a stream of people with all the necessary equipment—crystals, feathers, Frisbees, and more. They swarmed up the hill like ants. Chanting echoed off the canyon walls and the roadway was clogged with well-meaning, but not particularly helpful folks.

Next on the scene was the Press. They were excited about the sight and ready to write stories with dramatic headlines. Finally, last to arrive was the Park Superintendent. His intent, no doubt, was to try and bring sanity back to the mess, but alas, as he approached one of the buses, he slipped in the greasy mud in the bar ditch and fell flat on his fanny. Hurt only in pride, he pressed on with mud adorning his backside and I dared not laugh.

Eventually the park's front-end loader pushed the truck out of the way, everybody got back on the buses and the scene returned to as normal as it could, considering the situation. All in all, it was a perfect end to what the comic strip Doonesbury called "the moronic convergence."

The "moronic convergence" was a perfect finale for that crazy summer when a tornado lifted the top off my apartment and I watched as otherwise intelligent people crowded into Chaco Canyon and prayed to the spirits of Mother Earth and Father Sky.

- 20 -

Alibates Fire

Fighting fire is one of those ranger jobs that goes way back to the beginnings of the National Park Service. Traditionally, when a fire was reported all hands answered the call. However, beginning in the early '80s the Park Service began requiring those who fought fires to be certified. Proof of your fitness to fight fire was a "Red Card." At first, quite frankly, Lake Meredith and many other parks ignored the new requirement. When we had a fire, everyone turned out. But by 1987 the regional big shots put out the word that there would be hell to pay if the certification requirement was ignored and Larry made it clear that those without a card could no longer play. Consequently, that left the park with only John, Duane, Pete, and me to fight any fires.

John had invested a lot of time in training me to be a firefighter. But that was all I was—a grunt with a shovel or a Pulaski. My status changed when I got a call from the Chief to go to a fire up near the Alibates Flint Quarries National Monument, which was adjacent to and administered by Lake Meredith National Recreation Area. Our most qualified fire guy, John, was out recovering from knee surgery. I, Mister Nobody, was the best Larry had to offer at the moment. By being sent first to the scene I would be the initial incident commander, a scary thought to Larry I'm sure, but on the flip side, if it was a small fire I would have no one to command but myself.

It was a long way from the ranger station to the Monument. For the last ten miles of my journey I could see a large column of smoke coming from the ranch land next to the Park. That's when I realized this was a big fire. As I got closer I saw the fire was running towards the Park and would very soon be upon us. At this rate, several hundred acres would burn before anyone even began fighting it.

I radioed my report to the Chief and I was told to assume incident command. I was no where near qualified for such an important assignment. Fire fighting is serious business and people can die when mistakes are made.

As I entered the Monument along its wide dirt road, I saw a mile-wide fire front on the plains above me. The flames danced two to four feet high in the tall, dry grass and were approaching the canyon rim. If the fire stopped at the rim, it would quickly consume the light fuels and burn out. If however it dropped over the rim rock and started downhill, I would have a potential blowup in the making because on the slope and across the flats to the road the grass became taller and thicker. Grazing wasn't allowed on the Monument and the grass showed it. On the other side of the road, at my back, the flats opened up into the river bottom where the grass and brush were even thicker and the fire would be impossible to stop with the resources we had.

As I pulled up onto a little knoll I saw the fire stall in a few places and then start down the canyon slope. The Park Service's trailer fire pumps and few employees wouldn't even begin to make a dent in this fire. I radioed a report and requested every available fire engine in the area. Soon, multiple fire engines from Fritch, Sanford, Borger, and Potter County were on the way.

Because the flames aren't a hundred feet high, whipping through the crowns of trees faster than a man can run, the unwary can be tricked into a false sense that grass and brush fires are not dangerous. On this day, in my ignorance, I decided to purposely place my crew in front of the fire.

The road I was on cut straight across the fire's path halfway between the rim rock and the river. I reasoned I had to stop the fire before it made it to the heavy fuels and the road seemed to be the perfect place to make a stand. I staked out my command post at the top of a knoll at the far end of that long, straight road where I could see all the action.

The first firefighter to arrive was Duane with one of our trailer pumpers. I positioned him near me. The next arrival was a pitiful, homemade brush engine from Sanford and a couple of volunteers. I put them forty yards further down the road. One by one, additional engines arrived. The fire was now at the base of the canyon wall and beginning its run across the flats towards the road. Engines crews worked feverishly laying out hoses and getting ready for the battle.

My plan was daring. I knew that. What I didn't know was that if I had ordered a backfire to be set off of the road my plan would have been brilliant. By blackening the ground between the road and the oncoming fire I could have made a fire break and made the situation safe for the fire crews. But I was new and inexperienced so I waited for the fire to burn to the firefighters.

As the fire ran the last few feet to the road edge the flames suddenly surged up. A bar ditch paralleling the road was full of dry tumbleweeds and when the fire reached these fuels the flames shot skyward. In thirty seconds—in one short, violent act of rage—the grass and tumbleweeds flared up, flames rose ten feet high and curled over the roadway. Heavy smoke obscured everything except the closest engine—the tiny Sanford truck. Horror stricken and paralyzed by fear I watched as flames licked at the Sanford fire engine blistering paint and driving the firemen to seek shelter on the far side of their vehicle. I saw everything, but could do nothing.

Time stopped and I stood frozen. Then the flames banked down, the smoke cleared a little, and I could see down the line. All the engines were still there, their crews spraying water and killing the few flames left. The Sanford crew emerged from hiding and set to work trying to start their pump. Their near demise had been caused by a pump failure. All the others beyond my view had checked the flames before they were threatened.

It was some minutes before my heart slowed. I realized I could have been responsible for killing those men. No one had to tell me I had messed up; the saying, "God looks after babies and fools," came to mind.

The rest of the fire was anticlimactic. With the head lopped off, mopping up the body of the fire was routine. By dark only a few cowpies still burned. I stayed out all night to make sure the fire was totally out. Since this was the biggest fire to have occurred in the Park the successful outcome lessened my embarrassment for putting the fire fighting forces of the county in danger.

When it came to fires at Lake Meredith I could be incident commander in spite of my greenness. But outside the Park I was relegated to a job that matched my ability—firefighter only.

While the Forest Service, National Park Service, and Bureau of Land Management all have fulltime wildland firefighters, no one agency has enough to deal with all the large fires that occur each summer on public lands. To deal with them, a national mobilization takes place every year. Every agency commits people and equipment, and sends them wherever they are needed. This year, we were needed in Kentucky and North Carolina.

The first deployment was to a fire that kept the crew on its feet for a marathon thirty-six hours without a break. When it was finally over, the Forest Service put the crew up in a Holiday Inn. I slept for fourteen hours like a log. The next morning when I awoke and stepped outside my room I discovered crime scene tape stretched all around a room a few doors down. While I had slept, a shooting had taken place just a few feet away. I never heard a thing.

A day later, on a second fire, a fellow crew member accidentally bumped me with his razor sharp Pulaski. The result was a nasty cut to the back of my hand. Since we were in the middle of the woods, medical attention had to wait. I worked the rest of the shift with a bandaged hand and that evening the crew boss took me over to the local emergency room. A battleaxe of a nurse proclaimed that I had needed stitches but it was too late. She would clean the wound and tape it up. "Good!" I thought, until she pinned my hand down on a table top and went at it with a stiff brush.

The next day, our third fire, the crew was driven to a remote area—a jumping off point for a hike up the mountain. From the bottom of a deep and narrow valley I could see lazy puffs of blue smoke rising out of the forest above us.

I was readying my gear like everybody else when crew boss Jim told me that because of my injury I was to be left behind. I wanted to stay with the others—be part of the action. But Jim ordered me to "Just hang around here." Since a Forest Service truck had not yet arrived with promised juice and Gatorade, I suggested that I could bring the cold drinks up later. Doing anything was better than standing around all day. Because Jim could see that I was determined, he relented, saying he would flag the trail.

The crew "saddled up" shortly thereafter and marched away single file like a platoon of soldiers. Fire fighting is hard work and sometimes miserable work. But the shared adventure with its excitement, toil, deprivation, purpose, and accomplishment quickly blends a group of twenty strangers into a team. I wanted to be with my crew, my team.

An hour later, the Forest Service truck showed up. I loaded all the cans and bottles I could fit into my pack and then stuffed two more packs full of cans—one for each hand. I shouldered my pack, shifted the load, readjusted the straps, and picked up the two packs. Looking up the mountain, I saw the smoke was now rising in the warm morning air with more purpose.

Rather than going straight up the mountain to the fire, the local guide had said it was too steep. The only way in was to take an indirect route up a side drainage to the level of the fire and then traverse across the mountain to the fire.

I looked up at the smoke and then at the trail the guide had taken. The trail disappeared into the woods in a direction ninety degrees from the direction to the smoke. The crew's route was flagged and would be easier walking. I looked back in the direction of the smoke. The fire was close, less than a half mile away as the crow would fly. If there were no cliffs I was sure I could climb it, even loaded like a pack mule. I was no stranger to rough terrain. Growing up, I had been in and out of the Grand Canyon in places like S.O.B. Canyon and Lava Falls where there were no trails only rough routes. Even in Boulder City, I had many times climbed in and out of Black Canyon below Hoover Dam.

After a moments consideration I chose my route—a straight line for my goal. At first it wasn't too bad. The ground sloped steeply, but I could plod on slowly at my own pace. But as the incline grew, rest stops became a necessity and still further on, the pace became one of counting my steps and trying to make it to a hundred before resting. Then resting every fifty steps, next twenty and finally ten.

Soon, sweat stung my eyes and my shirt clung to me like a wet dishrag. Still the incline grew steeper. I could almost reach out and touch the ground in front of me while standing. My pace was reduced to slinging my two burdens ahead, stepping up a foot and pushing the packs ahead and doing it all over again. I watched for foot and hand holds. I lost track of time and distance; my world was only at my feet and the only time was now.

When I smelled the first wisps of wood smoke I knew I was close. Then I broke out of the brush at the foot of a creeping ground fire and I was all alone. Where was my crew? I called out. No answer. For an instant I wondered if there were two fires—was I at the wrong one? No, there had been only one smoke. Unbelievably, I had arrived before my crew.

Soon I heard the crashing of brush, the clanking of tools on rocks, and the scuffing of boots. I picked up my cargo, moved towards a place where I knew they must emerge and waited.

The first yellow-shirted firefighter out of the trees looked up with surprise. Grinning, I held out a cold pop and started my call, "Welcome ladies and gentlemen. Get your ice cold pop here, yes siree! Ice cold, step right up."

Fire fighting was hard work, but it was work that I truly enjoyed. When I was fighting a fire I was walking in the footsteps of my idol, John Riffey.

- 21 -

A New Boss

By the end of the long, hot summer, everyone was mentally exhausted and ready for change. Indeed, the end of August was the low point of the year. However, that summer of '87 it was not my weariness, but someone else's that changed my life.

John had been the Lake District Ranger for years. It had been non-traditional rangering and he'd finally had one too many boat calls. He was ready for a change. At the same time, Bob, on the north side of the lake, was also ready for a change. Together they concocted a plan to switch jobs and Bob became my new boss.

I liked Bob and welcomed him into boats, but I had one reservation, I knew he was afraid of the water. I wondered why he had ever agreed to the swap, but if this was what John and Bob wanted, then I would do my part.

And my part was to train my new boss. I had learned from my know-it-all, do-it-all stage the previous year that I had to be diplomatic. Even so, sometimes there was a fine line between my telling Bob what to do and providing instruction. Soon we came to sort of a workable arrangement: I took care of the routine boat patrols, he handled administrative matters and life was good for both of us. However, in my heart I knew this couldn't last.

There were few visitors to the lake during the winter, but with the coming of spring we would need all hands on the water. Bob had to learn how to operate a boat; our arrangement had to end. Bob and I started going out to practice when the weather was good. Then one cool and blustery spring day I informed Bob it was time he was introduced to rough water. He could see no logical reason why we would purposely go on the lake during such nasty conditions. It took some talking, but I finally convinced him he had to learn how to handle the boat in rough water. He knew, of course, that I was right, because most emergencies occur during heavy weather.

All morning long, Bob and I practiced maneuvering in the choppy waves. I would demonstrate and he would copy. We worked into the seas, ran with the seas, and turned our beam across the seas. We practiced coming up to a mid-channel buoy as if it were a person in the water needing rescue. I talked about how we would pull a person on board using various techniques.

When we began these practice exercises, the water was just right for training. But the wind built steadily and by late morning the lake was becoming uncomfortably rough. I decided we would take a break. We were near Blue West, a large side canyon, so we slipped into the harbor and sheltered water. Bob was already white-knuckles scared.

While Bob and I were sheltering up at Blue West, a group of sailboarders were enjoying the stiff breeze at the far end of the lake at Harbor Bay. They were a hardy bunch of sailors who always showed up anytime the wind blew. It mattered little to them that the water was cold enough to kill in minutes this time of year. Like most hardcore outdoor recreation enthusiasts, they gave little thought to potential risks and ample thought to pursuit of fun. But fun turned to trouble for one lone sailor who, moving with a quartering wind and sea, had traveled halfway across the lake and then attempted to turn and come back with the winds and seas in his face.

Fortunately, Ranger Wilson's patrol took him into Harbor Bay at that time. When he drove up, several visitors raced to his car and reported that there was a board sailor in trouble out in the lake. They said a lone sailor had gone out an hour before and when he tried to fight his way back, the waves repeatedly knocked him from his board. The witnesses reported that he had fought desperately, getting up and falling over and over.

Wilson saw a speck in the water that disappeared every time it sank into a trough. Because it would only be a matter of minutes before he lost him from sight, Wilson headed for higher ground and grabbed the radio mic.

Bob and I heard the call, "Two-Forty-Two where are you guys? We've got a board sailor down. About a half mile off Harbor Bay." Wilson never gave away emotion over the radio, yet I could tell he was concerned. Adrenaline surged. In one sense, all my time, all my training, all of my preparation at Lake Meredith was for this mission. Sure, we in the Lake District enforced boating laws, preached endlessly about safety, towed and jump started visitor's boats; but rescue was the ultimate purpose of our being on the lake.

I turned to Bob, who still clutched the helm. The color had drained from his face. He clearly knew what we had to do. We exchanged places and I took over the helm.

I pushed the twin throttles forward, the *Revenge's* bow rose up, white foamy waves trailing away from our stern and we lunged forward on our mission. Racing towards the junction with the main lake I could see monster white caps rolling past the mouth of Blue West. The waves had grown while we had been hiding in the harbor and were as big and bad as it gets on Lake Meredith.

We cleared the sheltering point of land and turned up lake into the angry, rolling seas. With the first wave our bow rose up with the sea, pointed skyward, then fell down, pointing to the bottom of the lake. Green water surged across the deck trying to hold the little bow down. But the *Revenge* was stout and she fought her way up, shuddering as she did so. Water sheeted off of our bow deck and flowed to the gunnels where it returned to the lake and the bow speared the next wave at its foot, as if we were to dive under it.

With each plunge, spray lashed at our windscreen and blew over the top of the boat, raining on us like a small cloudburst. I crouched down behind the glass to let the torrent pass over and then quickly stood to get my bearing again before the next wave. Our passage could have been less violent, but I was unwilling to slacken our pace for I feared it was not fast enough.

The *Revenge* was my favorite boat and I was glad she had been our choice for the day. She had brought me safely through my first big

143

storm, when Nancy and I had so pitifully failed, and now I knew she would deliver me again. And this time I was well prepared.

After a quarter of an hour we were at the point where the search would begin. Each time we came up on a crest I scanned ahead. Bob was doing the same. All I could see were endless, white, foamy caps and greenish gray waves. This was going to be Bob's first water rescue so as we pitched and rolled our way towards the scene I told him my plan. I had to shout over the roar of the wind, waves and engines. I was unsure how much, if any, of what I said was heard or understood. He didn't move or answer, but just kept staring ahead, intently looking for our target.

I radioed Wilson who was now on a high bluff overlooking the lake asking for directions. With his binoculars, Wilson could see the white form of the board sail and the black speck clinging to it. He answered, "I see him. He's about three hundred yards off of your port bow."

I looked but saw nothing. In these conditions a small target would be difficult to see. We would both have to be on a wave crest at the same time. I kept calling Wilson asking for course corrections. Without his eyes we could easily pass the victim and never see him. Rescue takes team work and Wilson and I had worked together many times.

"He's right in front of you," Wilson radioed. At that same moment I caught a glimpse of the board sailor as he rode over a crest. I yelled, "Bob, get ready, we'll take him on the starboard side." The victim was hanging onto his board but showed no sign of life.

Normally, when we would pick a man out of the water, we would stop short and throw him a line. In that way, especially in rough seas, we would be less likely to run over him with the boat. But this time, the victim was not moving and we had no choice but to pull close enough to reach him by hand.

Any mistake could cause serious injury to the person in the water and it was my turn to have white knuckles. I worked the helm with one hand and the throttles with the other. As each wave hit our bow it would yaw off course. I would ease the boat back and then we

144

would roll off again. Bob stood behind me at the gunnel, hanging on for dear life with one hand, and the other poised like a harpoon ready to hook the sailor as soon as he came within range.

When we were ten feet from the sailboarder he looked at us and I could see he was alive. Still he was making no effort to swim towards us. Even with his wet suit, the cold water was close to claiming him. I motored forward. Suddenly the boat yawed hard towards our victim. He disappeared under the flare of my bow. I pulled the port engine into full reverse. The bow swung back and the man popped out right beside me, his head at the level of my feet.

As I snapped the engines into neutral I shouted, "Grab him." Bob was already leaning far out over the side and his huge hand came down over the man. Bob was a big man and before I could turn around to help, he jerked the limp form out of the water and flopped him across the deck like a fisherman landing his catch. It wasn't graceful but it was quick. The sailboarder lay in the sloshing water that flowed from side to side as the boat rolled, alive but not by much.

I thought, "We've done it, we've saved him." And then my thought was cut off in midstream by Bob's voice. He bent over the man and roared, "God dammit man, what the hell are you doing out here!" Bob had been a trouper; despite his own fear, he had controlled his emotions until now. But now his fear turned to anger. I quickly turned away so my grin wouldn't be seen.

A short time later we motored into Harbor Bay where Wilson had an ambulance waiting. Our young sailor would live to sail again another day. I, on the other hand, was sure we would be buried at sea when Larry found out about Bob's angry tirade. Fortunately the incident never came up. Apparently the victim had been too out of it to remember the tongue lashing or he was too grateful to turn us in.

Bob, however, never fully recovered from the adventure. He knew he had made a mistake coming to boats and now he longed to go back to his beloved North District. As luck would have it, John got a transfer to another park shortly after that and Larry kindly let Bob return to his old job.

- 22 -

Second Chance

In 1985 I had been temporarily promoted to District Ranger. In 1988 I was once again promoted to temporary District Ranger. Because John left and Bob returned to his old district, I was the last man standing in the Lake District. As it had been in 1985, summer was coming and the Chief was short one district ranger. The difference this time was that I was qualified. I stepped easily and naturally into the position.

Every year since my arrival at Lake Meredith our water safety efforts had intensified. Our patrol hours had increased. Water safety slideshow programs were being presented at local businesses, schools, and service organizations. We were now inspecting boats before they launched and boats that were up to speed were given a decal to display. Over that same time period the accident rate fell.

But people were still wrecking their boats, injuring themselves, and occasionally dying. There was still room for improvement and now that I was District Ranger I saw this as my chance to make a real difference. Now I could do things my way.

I wasted no time getting started. Because patrol was the most effective way to make a difference, I made sure a patrol boat would be out every day and that there would be two out every weekend from mid-morning until after dark. I worked the late shift and Rod and Mike worked together during the day. By summer's end we had driven our water time up by a whopping twenty percent. We talked to more visitors, inspected more boats, and issued more warnings and citations than we had ever done before.

Since you can't push boats and equipment that hard without an intense inspection and maintenance program, I gave that task to the seasonal ranger, Rod. He spent many weekdays cleaning and repairing minor problems before they became major problems.

I put Mike, a school teacher who was a good speaker, in charge of our public relations efforts. He blitzed the media, working the local TV and radio stations, putting safety messages in people's utility bills, articles in the newspapers, and getting messages posted on highway billboards.

Summer 1988 was the culmination of years of effort. John, Nancy, Rod, and Mike all owned a piece of the season. The hundreds of hours of training, the thousands of hours at the helm, the tens of thousands of dollars in new boats and equipment, the neverending boat maintenance, the endless preaching about safety brought the Lake District to this moment in time, a golden summer and one I shall not forget.

There was however, a small incident that I would like to forget. Even though our national parks need law enforcement and even though this was a part of my job, I have never liked it. I enjoyed helping people and preventing accidents, but sooner or later, every law enforcement ranger who works in a high-incident park will have to use defensive tactics—tactics learned at the academy. My first time came during this, my fourth summer.

In a park with only six permanent field rangers, everybody has to pitch in when things get busy. One weekend when the Sanford-Yake rangers were backed up with calls, I volunteered to answer the call for a ranger at the swimming beach known as the Stilling Basin. This lifeguarded beach below Sanford Dam was a good place for families and it was always busy on the weekends.

On this day, a very intoxicated young man had created a disturbance by taking the rescue surfboard from one of the lifeguard towers and refusing to return it. Even though this was not my district, Dale, the seasonal ranger, and I took the call.

When we drove up we saw hundreds of people enjoying the day: swimming, playing in the sand, and picnicking. At first I couldn't see any disturbance, but the lifeguard pointed out the problem—a stout, young man playing at the water's edge. Since the young man did not appear aggressive, I told Dale to take the lifeguard up to my truck and get a written statement from her while I walked down to the water's edge to take care of the problem.

The young man saw me and staggered out of the water. Obviously he knew why I was there. He greeted me with slurred speech. I could see he was drunk and because I had learned that a folksy, friendly, and respectful style worked well here in west Texas, I returned his greeting in a friendly, unthreatening tone. I said, "Hey buddy, you can't take the lifeguard's board." Next I mentioned that he'd had too much to drink and told him to come up to my truck with me.

When we reached the truck I asked him a few questions and gave him several sobriety tests. The entire time he was cooperative and happy. When we were finished I said, "Well, you've had too much to drink and I'm going to place you under arrest." "Okay," he answered.

I ordered him to turn around and suddenly my cooperative drunk became belligerent. I spun him around, pushed him up against the truck, and reached for my cuffs. That was the moment everything changed. Mr. Friendly decided he was going to have no part of this.

What happened next reads like a comedy, but at the time it was not funny.

I levered one of his hands up into the small of his back and as I started to put the handcuffs on he screamed, "No cuffs!" He worked at a meat packing plant, a tough job, and his biceps were bigger than my legs. With apparent ease, he straightened out the arm I had drawn up to his back. Still hanging onto his wrist, I now used both hands to twist his arm up again. With a grunt, he once more straightened his arm and I knew I was in trouble.

He attempted to turn around. Being behind him was the only tactical advantage I had and I couldn't afford to lose it. He fought to free his arms and I fought back to maintain my limited control. Together we slid down the side of the truck towards the open cab door. The lifeguard sitting in the seat writing her statement screamed as we thrashed toward her. Then the fight reversed directions and we started sliding back towards the tailgate.

Out of the corner of my eye I saw Dale hopping up and down with his baton drawn. I yelled, "Hit him! Hit him!"

To strike a man either in anger or self defense is not as easy to do as TV would have you believe, especially for a first time, young seasonal ranger. I don't know whether the idea of seriously hurting another human being held Dale in check or if he just couldn't get a clear shot with all our wrestling, but he never swung.

As we reached the tailgate, Dale suddenly appeared with his handcuffs. With everything I had, I wrenched my opponent's arm up and Dale hooked one cuff over his wrist. The ratcheting cuff renewed the young bull's fighting spirit. He wildly tried to pull away. Now that one cuff became a potential weapon. No matter what, I knew I couldn't let go of it.

Down across the tailgate we rolled, the flailing more violent than ever. As we came to the far end, I saw my opportunity. I had him off balance; his legs were trapped by mine. With a mighty push I shoved us off the only thing holding us up, the truck, and we fell over like two trees crashing down in the forest, only I was the one on top, and I had his arms pinned so he couldn't catch his fall.

Slam! We hit the pavement, my fall padded by his body. His head bounced off the ground and for a moment he was stunned. I jumped astride of his back and click, click, click, the last cuff ratcheted home.

It was over. The entire battle probably lasted only a minute but I was exhausted. The sweat dripped down on my prisoner as I gasped for breath. When I finally looked up I was shocked to discover that I was surrounded by a ring of onlookers. Dozens of people had come to watch the fight, which now that I think about it, must have been pretty entertaining, but no one had attempted to help. Dale was there as well, grinning and apparently quite pleased with the outcome.

After all the trouble making the arrest, the trip to the Potter County jail, some forty-five miles away in Amarillo, was uneventful. The next morning I returned to the jail to pick up the young man and take him over to the Federal Courthouse for arraignment. When I walked into the jail I couldn't believe my eyes. His face was scuffed, swollen, black and blue. His head striking the pavement had been more severe than I thought. Even though my use of force had been appropriate and in fact, I would have been justified using more force in our hand to hand combat, I felt sorry for him. As I booked him out the jailer on duty gave me a wink as if to say, "Don't mess with the rangers, right?" Embarrassed I wanted to say no, that's not what happened, I was merely defending myself.

In court I got the same look from the magistrate. I'm sure the judge thought I had repeatedly hit the man with my baton. There was no way I could explain that I was simply doing my job and things got out of hand. I felt sorry for the young fellow and I felt even worse when it turned out that he was a nice guy when sober. He apologized repeatedly to me for any trouble he might have caused.

Other than that one little scuffle, the summer of '88 was a season I could be proud of. I didn't know this would be my last summer at Lake Meredith, but I'm happy to say I ended my stay with the knowledge of having accomplished my goal. I was now a fully qualified, competent National Park Service Ranger.

- 23 -

Going Home

While I was experiencing my best summer, a thousand miles away Yellowstone National Park was in the midst of the worst fire season on record. The entire country watched the fire on the nightly news broadcasts. Everyone was horrified at the prospect of the National Park System's crown jewel being destroyed. Repeatedly the call went out, "Send help!" Thousands of firefighters and National Guard soldiers poured into Yellowstone.

Lake Meredith sent seasonals and even though I wanted to be a part of the action, I felt that as the District Ranger my responsibility lay in my district. Then, during the first week of September, the call for help went out again. Yellowstone was still burning, and to make matters worse, seasonal rangers and firefighters all across the country were returning to colleges and universities. There was a desperate need for firefighters and with the busy summer season behind us, I volunteered.

I thought I was going to Yellowstone. I ended up in Utah. A big fire was burning in the Wasatch Mountains near Salt Lake City and the afternoon I arrived my crew went on night shift. The next morning we bedded down in a hot, dusty field thick with flies. Trying to sleep with the sun in your eyes and insects crawling over your face was next to impossible.

That evening I escaped the fly-infested field when my crew was bused north for the initial attack on a new fire near Ogden. We were directed to build a line up a steep canyon next to the flames and even though this was hot, smoky work, I found it much more exciting than the usual indirect approach.

The next day the plan was changed and we were helicoptered to a ridge above the fire. Now our task was to construct a fire line down the ridge, which would tie in with a line being built by crews coming up. Late in the afternoon we were told that we wouldn't be coming down for the night. Instead, we would be spiked out on the ridge. Spiking crews, that is having them camp on or near the fire line, was a common practice and while never pleasant, our campout was made worse because we didn't have our packs, sleeping bags, or extra food.

Just before sunset, the last helicopter of the day slung down a load of paper sleeping bags and some soggy sandwiches. After a poor excuse for supper we spread out in search of semi-level, semi-rock free ground for a place to sleep.

I chose a spot that at first seemed to have potential, but I soon discovered even a small rock sticking into your back is hard to ignore. As tired as I was, my discomfort wouldn't allow me to drift off to sleep. In the dark the constant crackling of our plastic ground covers told me my neighbors were also unable to sleep.

And then around midnight the wind hit. A front howled over the mountain ridge. My paper sleeping bag was pathetically thin and with teeth chattering, stomach growling. and ears ringing from popping and slapping plastic, I lay awake and prayed for sunrise.

With the arrival of the sun and its warmth my spirits revived. I even felt that I belonged to a special club—a club of men and women tough enough to face adversity and keep going.

After a cold breakfast my crew was assigned to build a line across a steep slope below a finger of fire. Twenty of us spread out, ten feet apart, heads down, backs bent. I heard but, intent on my task, ignored the sound of a chainsaw upslope.

All of a sudden a frantic yell snapped me to full attention. A log, a foot and a half in diameter and ten feet long, was rolling directly at me. The men in front and behind me dove back away from the butt ends of the massive rolling pin. For me there was no escape. In an instinctive act of survival I jumped straight up. The log caught me in mid-air and carried me backward, over a ravine's edge into the brush below. Miraculously the log passed beneath me.

At first I didn't move. How bad was I hurt? I felt no pain. Carefully I rolled over checking for broken bones. It seemed almost unbelievable, but I hadn't suffered anything more serious than some small abrasions above my boot tops. Like a cat, I had used up another one of my nine lives. Ten minutes later I was back on the line, telling lies, and making jokes about the incident.

After two weeks of long hours and backbreaking labor, the fire was contained and I was glad to get back to Lake Meredith. Gone were the hundred degree days and the madness of summer. Fall is a time when visitors are few and water fowl plentiful. It's when the park is for park rangers, my favorite time of the year. One cool, quiet day in October I sat on a rim rock overlooking the lake and took stock—asked myself questions. Where was I headed? Was I moving in the right direction? What lay ahead?

Eileen had graduated from law school the summer before and had taken the Texas Bar Exam. But neither of us thought of the Panhandle as our permanent home. After my successful summer as the temporary District Ranger I felt ready to move up the company ladder. Deep down I still dreamed of the Tuweep Ranger Station. I wanted to pick up were Riffey left off. But there would be little call for a lawyer there. Cows and coyotes never call for legal representation. So I applied to other parks, but selectively. Any future assignment would have to offer a promotion for me, an opportunity to practice law for Eileen (meaning no remote outposts) and be a "real" park.

Even though I was ready to move on, when the permanent Lake District Ranger position was advertised I put in for it. Confident in my qualifications, I was taken completely by surprise when shortly after submitting my application, I was summoned to the Superintendent's office and told I wasn't going to get the job. His blunt statement even before the selection process had begun struck me as extremely unfair. How could he dismiss me this way?

"But what if I'm the best candidate for the job?" I asked.

"You may well be, but you still won't get the job," was his terse reply. He then explained that when the park had filled the Sanford-Yake District Ranger job, Bob Wilson, a twenty-year veteran of the park had been selected. Bob had truly been the best man for the job, but one of the other candidates had filed a complaint with the Regional Office, alleging that the park had "wired" the job for their boy. The Superintendent had defended his pick but in the process had taken a good deal of heat for it. Now, he wasn't willing to do it again. He said it didn't matter if I came out number one, he would not pick me.

I thanked him for his brutal honesty. But when safely outside his office and out of his hearing, I gave vent to my anger with a string of descriptive, profane, even crude expressions. However, I had to give credit to the old man for having had enough integrity to tell me to my face what he was going to do. On the drive back to the ranger station my resolve hardened. I had just been informed I had no future at Lake Meredith, so I would go some place else. It was the push I needed to move on.

I really wanted to go to a park like Glacier, Mount Rainer, or Grand Teton but only Lake Mead and Lake Meredith had advertised openings. Since I had been told to forget about any advancement at Lake Meredith, I applied for the position at Lake Mead.

I knew, of course, that Lake Mead National Recreation Area is not one of the park system's jewels, but it is a major park. Located between the southern corner of Nevada and the northern corner of Arizona, its main attractions are two lakes: Lake Mead, created by the backwater from Hoover Dam on the Colorado River and Lake Mohave, created further down river by Davis Dam. More than 8 million people visit these two lakes each year where they enjoy boating, swimming, and fishing. Lake Mead is similar to Lake Meredith, but bigger—much bigger—and having lived and worked at Lake Mohave, I was aware of the park's pluses and minuses. While it wasn't my first choice, it seemed to be my only choice for advancement.

Then a month later, while waiting final word from Lake Mead, on a cold Friday in December the Chief called me into the office. When I arrived at headquarters, Larry, all smiles, ushered me into his office and, after the usual pleasantries about the weather, offered me the District Ranger job. I was stunned. How could this be? I had been told I would not get the job even though I was qualified and now it was being offered to me. Apparently John had changed his mind or Larry changed it for him, I never knew which.

However, it was my turn to drop a bomb. I said I needed time to think about this offer. Larry knew I had applied for a job at Lake Mead, and he knew they were considering me. Larry was a fair man and he told me to take a few days to decide.

Over the next couple of days I weighed the pros and cons. The job at Lake Mead was a promotion in grade but it was still only an area ranger position. Lake Meredith's job was a promotion and a District Ranger position. On paper Lake Meredith's was a better offer. But I could not forget the sting, the terrible disappointment, of being told by the Superintendent that I had no future at Lake Meredith. On the plus side, Lake Mead was close to a large metropolitan area—Las Vegas—where Eileen would be able to work as a lawyer. And Lake Mead did offer one other very important intangible benefit: it was home!

I called Lake Mead and explained to Jerry, the personnel officer, my dilemma; I wanted to come to Lake Mead, but I had a limited time offer waiting at Lake Meredith. How soon would they be making their decision? Jerry couldn't, or wouldn't give me a definite answer, but he did say their decision would be made soon.

I was faced with a problem—should I jump or should I stay?

- 24 -

Boulder Beach

Faced with the problem of should I jump to Lake Mead or stay at Lake Meredith—I jumped and immediately realized I had jumped out of the frying pan into the fire. My dream of walking in John Riffey's footsteps vanished the instant I walked into the basement ranger station at the Alan Bible Visitor Center.

Lake Mead is one of the busiest, roughest, and toughest parks in the National Park Service, and Boulder Beach is probably the roughest and toughest district at Lake Mead. Of course, being the new kid on the block, I was assigned to Boulder Beach, where I was greeted—not welcomed—by the District Ranger. I followed him through double doors into the dimly lit, cluttered, and cramped space that was to be my new home base. My superior pointed to a corner that was stacked almost to the ceiling with boxes and junk and said, "Find yourself a desk and chair and put it there."

This wasn't the welcome I had expected. So far, my first day, actually my first thirty minutes on the job, was a big disappointment. The District Ranger acted like my presence was an inconvenience. I would later find out he was irritated because my arrival had caused him to miss coffee with his buddies at the Lake Mead Marina.

I was still looking for a desk and chair when the dispatcher called to report a rollover wreck on the Kingman Wash road. Without missing a beat, my "welcomer" turned to me and said, "Go ahead and take that call."

Because I had worked at Lake Mead National Recreation Area before, I knew where the accident was, but at that moment I didn't even have so much as a pencil issued to me. Still in disbelief, I rounded up the things I thought I might need and headed out. As I drove to Kingman Wash I kept asking myself, "What the hell have I gotten myself into?"

A couple of days earlier, Eileen and I had pulled into the Boulder Beach employee housing area with our rental moving truck. We had gone east with everything we owned in a courier pickup, but the return home, five years later, required a little bigger truck. However, the twenty-foot van we rented was still less than half full.

For this assignment I was required to live in government housing. The three-bedroom, flat-roofed house looked sort of like something Frank Lloyd Wright might have designed on his worst day. However, it did have a couple of redeeming features—large picture windows and nice views. Lawn dotted with huge cottonwood and elm trees surrounded the house and from our back yard we looked out over the Lake Mead Marina and the beautiful blue water of Lake Mead. It wasn't a mansion, but for the first time Eileen and I felt like we had a real home.

But my first-day experiences made me wonder if I had a real job. I soon learned the job was real; too real. Boulder Beach was front-country hard-core law enforcement. Being the biggest district in the park, it had the biggest ranger staff, a whopping six field rangers. When spread out over two shifts with days off, vacation days, and sick leave, there were many times when only one ranger was on duty to deal with two large campgrounds, three miles of developed beach, two launch ramps, one huge marina complex, a store, a trailer village, dozens of miles of highway, and thousands of acres of surrounding back country and lake.

Within a month of my transfer to Lake Mead, a ranger shot and killed a murderer who was charging him with gun drawn just a few miles down the road from my house. Shortly after that, another Lake Mead ranger shot a drug-crazed man that was trying to stab him. I listened on the park radio to both of these events as they "went down" and felt my heart race as I imagined the emotional stress of firing at and killing another human being.

The hardness of this place was reflected in the rangers who worked here. Lake Meredith had been a friendly, happy place. The staff got along, worked together, and helped each other. They were all my friends. Boulder Beach, I would quickly learn was different. The stress, the heavy work loads, especially in the summer, fostered a survival instinct, a just-below-the-surface every-man-for-himself feeling. As the new guy I was constantly being judged by my peers. While I don't think anybody wanted me to fail, I was sure they were all watching to see if I would and there would be no helping hand should I stumble. Other than Bob McKeever, my immediate supervisor, no one bothered to show me around or teach me anything. If the District Ranger ever had something to say, it was usually criticism. My first year evaluation was based on a statistical print-out and the District Ranger's complaints that I didn't have enough arrests or enough tickets resulted in a less than stellar assessment.

While individuals remained aloof, the system immediately began to invest in me. Lake Mead needed its too few rangers to be highly competent in many areas. That spring I was sent to Advanced Boat Law Enforcement and Fire Apparatus Engineer School. I also received training in Hazardous Materials First Responder, Air Operations and Wildland Fire Crew Supervision.

Put in the context of baseball, Lake Meredith was the farm team and Lake Mead was the major league. While still learning this "big league" modus operandi I was called out one night to investigate "shots fired" in the Hemenway Campground. Another ranger and I drove to the campground without lights or siren and quietly parked at the entrance. The place was ghostly silent. After listening for a while, we started walking through the shadowy maze. At one point, as we stepped out of the shadows into the moonlight I saw my partner had drawn his revolver. I had felt no threat, but seeing his example, I silently slid my weapon out of the holster and held it down at my side.

The search of the campground was without incident and we returned to our vehicle without waking a soul. Since it was policy that anytime your weapon was drawn you had to document it, I asked my co-worker the next morning if he was going to write the report. He answered without hesitation, "I didn't draw my weapon." I knew I had a lot to learn; my law enforcement skills and instincts from Lake Meredith were insufficient here, but I vowed that, unlike my partner that night, I would always be by the book. If my "Dudley Do-Right," approach didn't work here, I would move on.

Starting around Easter weekend, visitation on the lake grew. The big weekend, just like at Lake Meredith, was Memorial Day. However, if I thought Lake Meredith was crazy on the summer-opening weekend, Lake Mead was overwhelming. The campgrounds were full, the parking lots were full, the beaches were packed, the launch ramps a snarled traffic jam, and boats buzzed everywhere.

That Memorial Day as I patrolled the beach, I saw a dozen people gathered around two young men in an all-out fist fight. As I drove up I held the radio mic, waiting to break into the continuous radio traffic to call in my location. The chatter continued, so I exited the patrol car without announcing my stop and rushed in shouting, "Ranger, break it up!"

I shoved the two men apart. As the two stood glaring at one another I stepped back and reached for my radio. Suddenly the man in front of me lunged forward and started beating the other one again. I tackled him from behind, drove him to the ground and was preparing to handcuff him when—WHAP! And then WHAP, WHAP! Turning I saw a woman striking me with her purse and screaming, "Let my nephew go!" I couldn't let go of the man to fend off the woman. However, in the background I heard approaching sirens and squealing tires.

The patrol car skidded to a stop and my co-worker emerged on the run. Like a linebacker, he put his head down and ran at full speed into the woman. The tackle sent her flying. "Holy cow!" I thought, "They play rough around here!" To me the incident was a big deal; to my co-worker it was a funny story to be told and embellished over and over.

My first six months at Lake Mead was an education. The place was tough and cold. Even though I would never be as cold as some, I had to measure up, show my peers that I was tough enough. That summer with each arrest made, each accident worked, each incident handled, I was accepted more and more as a Boulder Beach veteran.

- 25 -

Injured

In the Southwest the monsoon season begins in mid-July and with it the wildland fire season. Lightning from just one dry thunderstorm can start dozens of fires. Because of my fire fighting experience, when the call went out for hand crews, I was willingly recruited.

For my first assignment, I was bused to the Mogollon Rim country of Arizona. There, together with dozens of firefighters and a handful of bosses, I stood on a rock outcrop and stared at the steep, rough terrain below the rim. I could see smoke from the fire, but I also noted that the hike in would be hazardous, if not impossible. The brass reached the same conclusion and after a short pow wow decided to feed the crews and then bus us to the base of the rim and let us walk in from there.

When the chow line formed, I fell in for a long delayed and much anticipated breakfast. But as I stood in line, doing absolutely nothing, I felt something pop in my left knee and my leg folded under me. I landed in an awkward sprawl. Embarrassed, I tried to get up quickly, but when I straightened my left leg and put weight on it, a piercing pain racked my knee. Feeling ridiculous, I tried to laugh it off.

Certain it couldn't be anything serious, I told the crew boss I was okay. I said it was just a Charlie horse, and as long as I kept my knee bent I was able to minimize the pain. Even though I walked with a pronounced crooked-leg limp, I insisted that it was nothing serious.

After breakfast we were bused down to the base of the plateau. From there we had to walk several miles back up to the fire. By the time we were assembling our gear and getting ready for the hike up the mountain, my knee had become stiff and started to swell. I was secretly beginning to worry, but when the crew boss suggested I should stay at the base camp, I maintained that my knee was not serious and that I would walk it off.

The crew fell into line and I purposely took a position at the very back. I was afraid I wouldn't be able to keep pace with my bent knee stride but I soon discovered not only could I keep up, but when others fell out I was able to keep going. However, by the time we reached the fire it was obvious to me that my knee was not getting better. Seeing my limp, the crew boss told me to make a "helospot." The job of clearing a place where helicopters could lower supplies and equipment gave me a face-saving way to be relieved of the hard work of building a fire line.

I had finished the helospot and a helotack crew had taken over the duty of receiving sling loads, when an all-women Apache crew arrived. Because the Apache crew did not have radios compatible with the other crews (and I had a compatible radio) I volunteered to go with them as their radio man. For the remainder of the shift I worked along with the women and they showed me a whole new level of tough. Except for the crew boss, who spoke few words, no one talked, no one stopped, no one rested. The crew was like a digging, scratching, grubbing machine. When the shift was over, the women were the last ones to walk into the spike camp. They didn't complain even though by the time they arrived, all the semi-flat, semi-rock-free ground available for bed rolls had been taken by other crews.

The following morning, all the hand crews resumed fire line construction. I and one very sick Apache woman were left behind in camp with nothing to do. The division supervisor told me that a mule pack train was bringing in supplies and I would ride out with it when it headed down.

After a couple of hours, a firefighter passing through camp mentioned that the crews up on the line were out of drinking water. Bored and feeling useless, I decided to carry some water up to them. As I readied two 40-pound cubes of water for the trip I noticed the Indian woman was readying her cubes as well. Because she hadn't moved all morning I knew she was very sick and I tried to tell her to stay in camp. She ignored me.

Off we started, the lame and the ill, moving under the hot midday Arizona sun at a turtle's pace with our 80-pound loads. After an agonizingly long struggle, I looked up to see several crews in single file coming toward us. Thinking they were coming to help, we stopped and waited. But they walked right past us. I looked at my new friend and shrugged. As a second crew started past I asked, "What's up?" That's when we were told that the fire was making a run and everybody was falling back to a safe zone. Suddenly very tired, I sat down. The young woman also slumped to the ground. Our extraordinary effort had been for nothing. No one stopped for a drink, no one said thanks for trying, no one offered to help carry the water back down. As we watched the stream of yellow shirts go by I realized there were no familiar faces. The Apache and my crews had not come down. Should we retreat with the other crews or should we continue on? Since no one had ordered us to fall back, we decided to keep going. When we reached our crews they were hard at work, still fighting fire, thirsty and happy to see us. We lingered the remainder of the day with our respective crews.

That evening when we returned to spike camp, I was told someone from another crew with a sprained ankle had been given my place on the mule train going out. The following morning, my third on the line, my knee was swollen and painful and I knew it was time for me to seek medical aid. I told the crew boss I would walk out. He questioned my decision, saying there would be another mule train in the afternoon. He asked, "Are you sure?" I was definitely sure. I knew I had to take care of myself and if I waited much longer I might not be able to walk out.

The walk down was slow and painful. When I reached base camp I was amazed to discover that it had grown into a tent city with busy camp workers rushing here and there and dozens of fire crews coming, going, eating, and sleeping. I was quickly hustled off to the medical tent. The medics descended on me, taking vital signs, asking questions and probing my leg. But all I wanted was some aspirin, moleskin for my blisters, and sleep.

The next morning, a woman from the logistics section came over to the medical tent and said that I was going to be sent to a hospital in Payson for evaluation. I traveled in a Forest Service pickup to Payson where a doctor examined my knee.

That afternoon, sitting on the edge of the emergency room examination table in a Payson hospital, I watched my doctor examine the x-rays. He kept saying, "hmm"—never a good sign. Finally he turned to me and explained. The end of the femur had crumbled and bone fragments were in the knee joint. It would take surgery to fix the problem.

The Forest Service, my employer of the moment, arranged for me to see a specialist in Phoenix the next day. The following day I was in surgery. Fortunately, my brother Dave lived in Phoenix and I stayed with him for a few days until I was finally flown home.

Summer was in full swing, but I was benched and missing the action. For two weeks I hopped from the bed to the couch and back again. The days were long and boring. To help pass the time I listened to the park radio but it didn't help. Every time my peers rolled on a call I wanted to go too.

With Eileen working as a law clerk and studying for the bar exam, which she would take in October, I found home to be lonesome as well as boring. Incidentally Eileen passed the bar exam and became a practicing attorney, working first in family law and later in the field of construction defects.

After a couple of weeks the doc gave me the okay to go back to work on light duty. This meant sitting around the ranger station rather than at the house. On my first morning, just as I checked on duty at 6 a.m., the dispatcher asked me to respond to an assault call at the lodge. I explained that I was still on crutches and unarmed, but I volunteered to check it out. The dispatcher promised backup.

At the lodge I learned that an employee had discovered an indigent sleeping behind the building. When rousted out, the man had grabbed a two-by-four and started swinging. Even though I was unarmed and no match for a man with a two-by-four I hopped out of the office to confront this vagrant. Suddenly the attacker came around the corner. I pointed my crutch at him and shouted, "Stop, you're under arrest."

I still laugh when I remember how the man obeyed my command. Maybe he thought any damned fool making an arrest on crutches was nobody to mess with. My backup arrived, hooked him up, took him away, and I returned to the ranger station to write the report. When my boss learned that I had arrested a vagrant armed only with a crutch, he told me if I pulled a stunt like that again I would be home watching "All My Children" until my hair turned gray.

The healing process was slow. August gave way to September. Not allowed in the field, I desperately needed something to occupy my time. The unfinished Boulder Beach Fire Station was a short distance from our house. Every day as I hobbled restlessly about my front yard I would look at this big shell and think, "Why doesn't someone finish it?" It had been built over a year before; materials for the interior had been purchased and were stacked inside. Since I was not allowed out in the field and I hated hanging around the ranger station, I volunteered to finish the fire station.

I'm not sure how "light duty" the framing and carpentry was, but the boss approved it. During the next month I spent my days completing the building. When done, the place took on the look of a real working fire station.

As I healed, I mistakenly believed everything would be fine. However, on my final follow-up visit with the orthopedist, he dropped the bomb. I would have to change my lifestyle. My knee couldn't take any pounding—no running or jumping. And, the doctor added, that someday I would have to have a knee replacement. I could, of course, postpone the knee replacement by avoiding pounding activities.

I still thought everything would be fine. I would quit running for fitness. I would ride a bike. As far as the job went, I would give up fire fighting and avoid the "heavy lifting" on search and rescue calls. Fire fighting was voluntary duty and there were lots of support jobs on search and rescue call outs. I didn't have to always be the one in the field climbing mountains and carrying the litter.

When I reported the doctor's cautions to the District Ranger, the reaction was not at all what I expected. There was no understanding, no willingness to make allowances. Word came down from headquarters: I would do my job, all of my job, or I would be out of a job. It was disappointingly apparent to me that after all of my dedication and loyalty to the Park Service, if I was damaged goods, the system would throw me away. I had naively thought my leaders were different.

Understanding now that a bureaucrat could take away my dream, I decided I would not let that happen. I called the orthopedist and explained the situation. I told him I needed a letter saying I was 100% fit for duty. The orthopedist understood and gave me the letter I requested.

I had asked for very little in the way of consideration from Lake Mead but since they were unwilling to work with me, I would work around them. I couldn't be forced to go out on fires, and in fact, the park actually preferred that I didn't. As to SAR missions and any other rough activities, I knew I could find ways around that too. The real issue was that by saving my career I had sacrificed my qualifications for any future medical claims. The doctor had made it clear that someday I would have to have replacement surgery. When that day came I would be on my own.

- 26 -

This Place Can Be Nasty

It is hard to overstate how intense it could get at Boulder Beach. In a national magazine article, Lake Mead was ranked as the sixteenth most dangerous park in the nation. We were right up there with the big urban parks like New York City's Central Park. And during the spring and summer of 1990 it lived up to its reputation. Partly because we were short handed and partly because I tended to be gung ho, I racked up a record for the number of middle of the night call-backs. I had three times more call-outs than anyone else. There were nights I would get up two and three times to deal with wrecks, drunks, and fights. The worst of the call-outs came one night when a young man and woman camped on the beach were attacked by two armed thugs. While the assailants held the man at gunpoint, the two took turns raping the woman. This case would later appear on the television show, "America's Most Wanted."

My second Memorial Day at Lake Mead made the first look like child's play. Once again, all hands were put on twelve-hour shifts and I drew the afternoon and night shift. By this time in my career I had no understanding of or compassion for drunks. They were, as far as I was concerned, a fight, drowning, or motor vehicle accident waiting to happen.

On this Memorial Day shift I made three trips into Las Vegas to book a drunk into the city jail. It took at least three hours to drive into Las Vegas, book the drunk, and complete the necessary reports.

It was midnight when I returned after my third trip. Entering the park I radioed David, a young, still green but dedicated ranger, and

171

told him that I was going to stop by the ranger station to set the alarms and we could call it a day. He said he would meet me at the parking lot.

However, we didn't call it a day because a few minutes later, David radioed me that he had come upon a roll-over vehicle accident with one victim unconscious and trapped in the car. As I called Rescue Four, our volunteer ambulance crew, I remember thinking "Will this day never end?"

The accident was on the Horsepower Cove road. A speeding vehicle had failed to make a curve and now a young man was fighting for his life. The ambulance crew called for the medical evacuation helicopter and a short time later we loaded the victim into the helicopter.

As quickly as the helicopter had appeared, it disappeared into the black night. The rush was over and I was suddenly very tired. All I wanted to do was wrap up the investigation and go home. David and I hastily interviewed witnesses, photographed the scene, studied the roadway marks and recorded pertinent data. Speed, not thoroughness, was our motivation. Once finished, I signaled the tow driver that it was all his and sat down on the side of the road to rest a minute. As I sat there, one of the Rescue Four technicians said he didn't think the victim was going to make it and right then I was sure we were in for trouble.

Because fatal accidents are almost always subject to civil and/or criminal litigation, a thorough and detailed investigation is required. But our investigation had not been thorough or detailed. Totally exhausted, I had rushed the investigation and I knew my efforts weren't up to standard. Nevertheless, I could do no more.

As for the young victim, he did die, but apparently our investigation was good enough, for I never heard anything more about the case. There were plenty of incidents that summer, but unless someone died it was considered pretty much routine.

However, not every emergency turned out bad. There was one event that had a happy ending. This incident happened on a hot summer day when I was showing David how to dock a boat. We repeatedly pulled the Skipjack patrol boat up to and then backed away from the Government Dock at the marina. Glancing up from this task,

I saw a thin, black column of smoke rising from the center of the marina.

The close side-by-side mooring of hundreds of flammable boats makes the possibility of a huge fire real. There was no activity near the smoke, which meant it had not yet been discovered.

David quickly spun the Skipjack around and we headed for the fire. As we motored deeper into the marina, we saw the source of the smoke—a decrepit-looking old wooden cabin cruiser. Smoke was seeping out around the seams, windows, and hatches. We saw no flames, but the glass was black with soot and nothing could be seen inside the main cabin.

We pulled into a nearby slip. Immediately, several marina employees arrived with a portable fire pump and hose. They set up their equipment, started the pump and began washing down the back of the cabin. However, the fire was inside the boat and the stream of water hitting the outside of the cabin was wasted effort. I radioed for the Boulder Beach fire engine. I knew when the crew arrived they would be suited up in turn-out gear and breathing apparatus—equipped to enter the cabin to find and put out the fire. There was really very little we could do except move adjacent boats away and wait for the fire crew's arrival.

However, I'm not one to wait for help. I had to do something. As the district's fire chief I knew better, and would have criticized anyone else for doing what I did, but I climbed onto the bow of the cruiser and shouted for the marina crew to pass the fire hose over to me. Then I called for the marina boys to force the cabin door open. I figured the open door would create a vent for the smoke and fire gases while at the same time I would force the bow hatch. I would spray water down into the hull and create an air flow pushing the smoke out the rear cabin door. This action would render the compartment safer for the fire crew. If I was lucky I might even get a little water on the fire itself.

The marina employees forced the cabin's rear door open with an axe. As it swung wide, hot, thick, black smoke billowed out, driving the men back. On the bow I pried up the deck hatch. After a stubborn moment it gave way with a snap and smoke poured out. I shoved the nozzle into the black cloud and shot water into the interior. Within seconds the stream reversed the flow of smoke. When the smoke began to clear I lay on my stomach, leaned over the hatch, and directed the water aft. The air in the forward compartment gradually cleared. Still no flames were visible and I was able to see the interior. Directly below the hatch was a bunk and on the bunk was a victim—a kitten.

Sprawled out in a death posture was a tiny, wet, limp, furry body. I yelled to Dave that I was going in, and before he could object to such a foolish act, I dropped through the hatch. Still directing the fire hose with one hand I scooped up the little form in the other and passed him up and out through the hatch. David carefully took the lifeless animal from me.

I was about to turn and climb back out when I realized the atmosphere in the compartment was quite tenable. Because the water stream directed aft was pulling fresh air in through the hatch and pushing the smoke out the cabin door, I decided to stay and look for the fire. The air cleared and I saw the overhead burning in the next compartment. Alternating between spraying the ceiling and spraying out the rear door, I knocked the fire down and continued clearing the smoke. That's when I found a second victim—a dog. He was crouched down on the deck, terrified, with bad burns on his back. Dropping the hose, I picked him up and carefully carried him out of the cabin. As I emerged into the bright sunlight I could see the engine company coming down the dock, heavily laden with their equipment and tools.

I handed the dog off to someone in the crowd and then looked toward our patrol boat where I saw David down on his knees stooped over the kitten. He held an oxygen mask over the kitten's face with one hand while lovingly caressing the matted fur with the other. I couldn't believe it—the kitten was alive. Later that day, Dave told me the kitten was not breathing when I handed him out, but he improvised—found a way to give the little fellow mouth-to-nose respirations until he began breathing on his own. Both the dog and kitten survived and David and I will forever share that special feeling that comes from saving someone, even if that someone is furry.

- 27 -

Return to Shivwits

One hot afternoon late in the summer of 1990, a fisherman named Stephen and his friend went out on the lake in their small fishing boat. They motored across the lake and wet their lines on the east side of the Boulder Basin. It was monsoon season and by mid afternoon, large thunderheads appeared overhead and grew rapidly. Unmindful of the danger, they continued to fish as the threat developed.

At this same time, I was on boat patrol in the area. I saw the dark and ominous thunderheads building, but remained on the lake because I felt safe in the *Major Powell*, our largest patrol vessel, and also because Ranger Bob at Lake Meredith had taught me "when others come in, you go out." I knew this was a time when I might be needed.

Soon a localized, short lived, violent storm hit. The rain pelted, the wind howled, and white caps pitched the *Major Powell* as I motored along slowly, searching for any vessels in distress. Within thirty minutes, it was all over and I headed back to the Government Dock unaware that the storm had sunk the small fishing boat, probably not more than half a mile from where I had patrolled.

Stephen's friend, the survivor, was plucked from the water by a passing sailboat and the Park Service was alerted. I rushed back to search the water, but Stephen was gone. I never saw a face, never retrieved a body, but I could not forget this tragic accident. Even though I tried to put this catastrophe behind me, I kept remembering his friend's anguished voice as he talked about the accident, repeating the name— Stephen—over and over.

Never really a hard core law dog and haunted by memory of this and other tragic accidents, I was mentally worn out by the end of summer. I had good reason to feel exhausted, because my end-of-year evaluation showed that I had racked up the highest number of visitor contacts, boat patrols, backcountry patrols, emergency medical calls, and the widest range of law enforcement calls in the Lake Mead National Recreation Area. I had taken dozens of violators to jail and worked almost two hundred significant incidents. In short, I had given it my all and I was ready for a change.

Fortunately for me, several months earlier the District Ranger transferred to headquarters and Ranger Bob McKeever moved up to take his place. That left Bob's old job, a GS-9 position, vacant and created an opportunity for promotion. I applied for this position, which was a step up in grade. Since Bob had been the district's backcountry lead, it was rangering closer to my heart. I longed to do more traditional work and less front country patrol.

That fall I was notified that I had been selected to fill this position. Ironically, I received word of my promotion shortly before I was to leave for hunting patrol at Shivwits where my ranger career had begun. I say ironically, because the timing was unexpected, yet perfect. At the moment when I was suffering law enforcement burnout, I was given a career change and a short assignment to Shivwits where I could recoup.

When I had shut the gate and driven away from the fire camp almost ten years before, I had not expected to ever return. Being selected to participate in a joint Arizona Game and Fish/National Park Service deer hunting patrol meant I could return "home" for a few weeks.

As we drew closer to *my* ranger station—the Shivwits fire camp—I became more and more excited. Each turn in the rutted, dusty road was familiar. As we bounced along I would recount: here is where I had a flat, here is where I got stuck, here is where I found that big old rattlesnake and on and on. My time at Shivwits had been very special and I was looking forward to reliving it. Nearing the end of our journey I strained to see through the trees, to see again the large meadow and the buildings of the Shivwits Ranger Station nestled under the ponderosa pines on the far side of the valley. And then I saw it. In the distance across the valley I saw the log fence, the Butler garage, the water tank tower, the cache, and the trailer; I felt the joy of a homecoming.

But as we drew even closer I saw it was not the same. Approaching the gate, the joy drained from my soul. It was not as I remembered. It was not *my* ranger station. The dreadfully inadequate trailer with its mice and no plumbing or heat was gone; in its place stood a modern mobile home. Most of the log fence had been torn down. The Witte generator was gone and the ranger station office at the end of the porch—the one I had built with my own hands—was gone. Someone once told me you can never go home again; as a profound sadness washed over me I learned the true meaning of those words. However, the blue funk didn't last. It was still good to smell the pines again and taste the clean air. It wasn't my ranger station anymore, but it was still my Shivwits.

The next day, Roy and I began our hunting patrol duties. We contacted the few hunting parties camped in the area, checked their licenses, and more importantly got to know them. Ninety-nine percent of all hunters are good people, who love the outdoors and would never knowingly do anything wrong. For those guys our job was only to make sure they knew all the park rules and where hunting area boundaries were. Grand Canyon National Park was off limits, but they were unlikely to go there since in most places, that first step was a thousand feet straight down.

Our real purpose was to watch for any of the one percent who couldn't play by the rules. There are always a few who think the rules don't apply to them and that they won't get caught. But only one hunting group, camped just outside the park, appeared to need watching.

Each day after dinner we gathered around the campfire and told stories and lies. I shared my fire fighting misadventures. I chuckled as I told how in the dark of night after seeing bear tracks one day I had imagined my dog Dingo was a bear. I talked about my comedy of errors, but withheld my most precious memories, because I knew no one could understand my feelings.

One evening after supper I went for a walk. Without consciously directing my steps I walked toward the place where Eileen and I had fought our first fire. After a time I came to a ponderosa lined draw that felt right. I knew I was close and, after a little meandering, I came upon the old burn scar. I followed the edge of the burned area until I found what had drawn me to this place—a rock with a tiny name scratched onto it—"Eileen." The name, nearly erased by time, was still there—a testament of my love for my bride. I know the Park Service, with good reasons, has rules against such behavior and I wouldn't do it again, but seeing that rock made me smile. Here at Shivwits, in a house trailer with dozens of mice, Eileen and I had begun our married life. This would always be my sacred place.

In fact the entire Arizona Strip is special to me. It is where my brother and I spent our summers visiting Grandma and Grandpa Craig. It is where I met my role model, Ranger John Riffey.

Our hunting patrol that fall was without incident except for one violation. I saw a hunter shoot from the road, which is a no-no. Because the offense took place outside the Park, the game warden issued the citation. The event would have been long forgotten but the hunter decided to plead not guilty, a trial was set and I had to appear as the witness.

I had testified in court dozens of time before, but court on the Arizona Strip was a new and interesting experience. A park plane flew me to Colorado City, a small polygamous Mormon town on the Utah-Arizona boarder. The game warden I was testifying for met me there and we drove to Moccasin, a tiny community. Expecting a typical court house, I was surprised when we turned off the lone asphalt road and onto a dirt road. At the end of a half mile long two-rut drive we came to a small house. "We're here," the game warden announced. Here was clearly someone's home and the only sign that anything official was going on were the highway patrol cars parked in the front yard.

A woman wearing an apron answered our knock and invited us in. We joined half a dozen men—some witnessing and some accused—

in the living room. After telling us to make ourselves at home and to turn on the TV if we wanted to watch it, the woman disappeared into the kitchen. A short time later she reappeared with a plate of cookies.

Periodically the judge would call out from somewhere in the back of the house and a new group would head down the hall. Finally it was our turn. Court was in a small bedroom. In fact the room was so tiny that the judge sat behind a desk; in front of and abutting the desk was a table where the prosecution and defendants sat. There was one chair off in a corner, where I presumed the witness sat. With little pomp, court began. I told what I saw, the defendant told his story, the judge asked a few questions and then ruled: pay a fine, probation for a year, and who's next? That was by far the best court experience I ever had and, while I generally disliked going to court, I would gladly return, especially if it was baking day.

- 28 -

Training

One of the great things about being a ranger, other than working outdoors in some of the most beautiful places in the world, is that the job is so varied. Tedium should never be a problem for anyone with a little hustle. A ranger wears many hats and there is always something to do.

Most people think of the ranger as a naturalist, who leads hikes, mans the entrance stations, and gives campfire talks. But rangers do much more. In some parks the emphasis is on protecting and preserving the special features, man-made or natural, of the park. In such places the ranger wears the hats of a scientist, historian, archaeologist, wildlife biologist, or geologist.

But at Lake Mead the emphasis was on visitor services and protection. Here, the most important hat was policeman. Also on the hat rack were emergency medical technician, firefighter (both structural and wildland), boat operator, and search and rescue specialist. As I started up the company ladder, I was also expected to wear the hats of planner, safety expert, and supervisor/administrator.

The variety of the job required constant and continued training. My education had begun many years before when I reported to Lake Meredith. At first my training focused on fundamental skills, but later in my career the training was specific and advanced. At Lake Mead my classes included training for structural fire officer, advanced boat accident investigation, man tracking, hazardous materials spills management, aircraft ditching survival, and, my most favorite subject, technical high angle rescue.

Lake Mead had an all volunteer technical search and rescue (SAR) team. The group was composed of a few rangers and park maintenance employees, plus volunteers from Boulder City and Henderson Fire Departments and Las Vegas Metropolitan Police Department's SAR Unit. I met with this team twice a month for training. One Saturday a month we would head into the field and perform a rescue problem, such as raising or lowering a victim over vertical terrain.

During my training I progressed from student to teacher. I taught map and compass classes, basic seamanship (with Bob McKeever, the park boating officer), and structural fire fighting classes. I tried to make drills as realistic as possible. For fire fighting we practiced responding to make-believe fires: pulling hoses, setting up ladders, and conducting mock victim searches by crawling through buildings with blacked-out face masks. Once I even took a group through live burn exercises in the City of Las Vegas's fire department smoke tower. The young rangers loved it; the older ones hated it.

Within the Boulder Beach District was a water treatment and pumping plant that provided the lion's share of water for all of Clark County and Las Vegas. Because the facility used massive amount of liquid chlorine, I included sessions on handling chlorine leaks as part of the training program.

Unknown to anyone except the District Ranger and the top managers at the water treatment plant, I set up a drill that simulated a catastrophic chlorine leak. My phone rang at six in the morning on the day of the planned exercise. Before I could answer the phone, it stopped ringing and I went back to bed. Minutes later there was a heavy pounding on my front door. Still half asleep, I staggered to the door and opened it a crack. Dave, the ranger living next door, pushed the door open, shoved my fire helmet at me and shouted something about a big chlorine leak. Of course, I thought some idiot had gotten the drill time wrong. It couldn't be a real chlorine leak. But it was. A huge chlorine gas cloud hovered over Henderson. Now what are the chances of a major chlorine leak on the day we were planning to have a chlorine leak drill?

However, the leak was at one of the chemical plants in Henderson and was managed by the Clark County and Henderson Fire Departments. We were sent to backfill for Boulder City Fire Department and handle any city calls that might come in while they were helping Henderson. So while other fire departments were evacuating thousands and treating dozens of people for symptoms of chlorine inhalation, my engine saw no action. But had we been needed, we were prepared.

My boss, Bob McKeever, believed rangers should be prepared for whatever hat they were asked to wear and he was especially concerned that rangers new to the district be given extensive training and orientation before they were sent out into the field alone. The way I had been introduced to the district was not the way to do it and Bob took steps to correct this inadequacy. Years later the Park Service would adopt a Field Training Program for new rangers, but in 1991 Boulder Beach was ahead of its time.

That spring two new rangers were hired and I was selected to train one of new recruits—Jim Sanborn. Jim was by no means a rookie, but Lake Mead was rough and tumble and it only made sense to provide training. During Jim's orientation period he and I worked together and I soon realized Jim was by far the most squared away ranger I had ever met. Just a few years younger than me, he and I discovered we had a lot in common; during exciting, busy nights of training in May 1991 we became lifetime friends.

Bob McKeever put us on the night shift to maximize Jim's exposure to the district. Together we patrolled roads, beaches, and campgrounds. I introduced Jim to emergency medical technicians, tow truck drivers, and anyone he might need to call upon in the performance of his job. Because I wanted Jim to know medical helicopter evacuation and jail booking procedures, we rushed to every incident. I wanted Jim to know everything about his new district—to see it all and do it all.

One night when there had been little action, I decided Jim and I should check out Saddle Cove where we were almost certain to find trouble. We parked the patrol car near the entrance to the area and walked in, because the only way to effectively patrol the area is to get out of the car. On foot in the dark we could move about undetected and observe everything that was going on.

On this night, we immediately found a group smoking marijuana. We stepped into the campfire light and announced our presence saying, "Good evening, Park Rangers." Everybody was gathered up around the fire and patted down. While I watched and visited with the group, Jim seized baggies, bongs, and pipes. Out of the corner of my eye I kept track of Jim, because even though he was a competent and experienced ranger, his previous parks had been quieter and more traditional. What we were doing was new to him.

All of a sudden, my portable radio came to life with these words, "All units, we have a murder in progress at Saddle Cove." We were in Saddle Cove! My excite-o-meter went from zero to a hundred. I reached for my revolver's grip. Listening for the sounds of screaming or gun shots, I stared into the darkness and I called out to Jim. With a "murder in progress" it was time to forget the marijuana arrest.

Saddle Cove isn't that big of a place and I knew the "murderer" couldn't be very far away. We ran back to our patrol car, Jim still toting an armload of contraband. My thoughts were racing ahead faster that my feet could carry me.

Fortunately, by the time we reached the car the dispatcher had more information and the report of a murder in progress had been wildly exaggerated. It turned out to be just another gun call—a drunken fisherman threatening some obnoxious teenagers with a gun over disputed territory. At Lake Mead such calls were not unusual. I took a number of these calls each season.

It had turned out to be no big deal, but the initial dispatch rated as an all time number-one, heart-stopping call. While I fancied myself as a journeyman ranger, this event reminded me that Lake Mead could still pitch me some curve balls. My own education was always a work in progress.

- 29 -

Backcountry

Bob McKeever believed backcountry patrol and resource protection were on equal par with front country patrol and visitor services. Therefore when he became the District Ranger he put me in charge of boating and backcountry. My early training and experiences at Lake Meredith had instilled in me a passion for boating and backcountry work was close to my vision of ideal rangering

Bob spelled out his agenda: patrol and manage the backcountry aggressively, build and maintain roads and trails, supervise camping and hunting, and bring the rampant off-road vehicle use to an end. These were tall orders and I was given a two-man crew.

Immediately we stepped up patrols in places that had been visited before only infrequently. We worked the desert bighorn hunt, contacted every group of hunters and went over the rules with them thoroughly. We walked the remote shorelines around the lake and checked fishing licenses.

Off-road vehicles of all types were coming out of urban areas, crossing the surrounding desert, and spilling into the park causing massive damage. Bringing off-road vehicle use to an end became our number one priority. Patrol alone wasn't going to do it. The chances of being in the right place at the right time were not in our favor. The district had well over fifty miles of exterior boundary, much of which was adjacent to or easily accessible from urban areas. Signs along the boundary were not stopping these motorcycle and all-terrain vehicle riders. What was needed was a physical barrier. So beginning in the fall of 1991 and continuing each off season until I left the district, the Backcountry Unit built fence.

We packed to the fence line every post, every roll of wire, everything needed without the aid of vehicles. We drove every steel post with a post-pounder by hand and stretched the wire tight like guitar strings with muscle power. For me fence building was ranger work, doing what was needed to be done to protect the park. My years at the family ranch had prepared me well for the job. There were other rangers in the district who tried to avoid anything to do with the backcountry, but I was more than happy to have the job all to myself. That fence—strong and neat—was my pride.

I also drew great satisfaction from exploring the wilderness areas of the district. The desert is an amazing place of magnificent contrasts, stark in the macro-view, with vistas measured in dozens of miles. Geology and time are exposed for all to see in naked mountains, canyons, alluvial slopes, and playas. But in the micro-view, the desert is just as amazing with many varieties of cactus, animals from kangaroo rats to mountain lions, and an artist's entire palette of colors in the rock outcrops. I walked the canyons and ridges. I made it my mission and the mission of my crew to know the backcountry well.

One day as I was patrolling a road in Goldstrike Canyon, miles from Boulder City, I came upon a middle-aged man. I stopped to check on his welfare and that was the beginning of a long friendship. Mike was retired and he loved the desert. He had spent many days hiking the district's backcountry and I immediately recognized that he would be an asset to my operations. I gave him the VIP (Volunteer in Parks) speech and a few days later he signed up. Not long after that his brother, Spike, joined as well. I already had three other VIPs working for me and with all this help, the backcountry unit started making some serious headway.

One of the areas Bob wanted addressed was trails. The park had a plan showing miles of routes. But it was all just a paper exercise, for the reality was that the park had only a few miles of maintained trails. Many of the proposed trails were in the Boulder District and Bob wanted to make them a reality.

Two of my VIPs, Hank and June, were improving an existing informal trail from the campground to the visitor center. With the recruitment of Mike and Spike, I now had the manpower to tackle Bob's big dream—a wilderness trail of some forty miles that would run from the Alan Bible Visitor Center to the Nelson highway. The route was along the western rim of the Colorado River canyon. Much of it was along ridges and over peaks that looked down on the green ribbon of the Colorado River below. It was extremely rugged country, but beautiful in its harsh wilderness.

Mike and Spike spent months exploring the rim, walking every possible route. As they completed each section, Jim Sanborn and I would hike their recommendations. The crunch of gravel underfoot, the creak of pack straps, sweat on my brow, the rhythmic breathing, the wonderful feeling of exertion reminded me why I became a ranger. As I walked along the skyline with the silent Colorado to my left and the forever vista of basins and ranges to my right I felt the great satisfaction of being a traditional ranger.

But the peace of wilderness was sometimes interrupted by distress. It happened early one morning when I got a call from Dispatch telling me to meet the park pilot, Bruce, at the airport for a flight over Shivwits. An airplane flying to Grand Canyon had reported that there was a group of people near the fire camp signaling for help.

When we arrived, we saw below us a group of a dozen or more people on the road to the camp. On the ground the word "help" was spelled out with rocks. A tarp was spread over a small mound nearby. Immediately I knew there was a body under that tarp. Bruce circled the plane back for another look.

Years ago there had been a dirt airstrip in the sage flats in front of the fire camp, but it had been abandoned long before I had worked at Shivwits ten years before. What was once a cleared, marginal strip was now pockmarked with clumps of sage and grass, dotted with stone-hard cowpies, undermined by gophers, and occasionally criss-crossed with small washes. Bruce swooped down and skimmed a few feet off the ground over the proposed runway. At the end of the run he announced, "I can land."

The landing was bumpy, dusty, and scary. While Bruce checked out the plane I walked to the group several hundred yards away. It was just as I suspected. Under the tarp was a body of a teenage girl.

The group made up of several adult leaders and a handful of teenagers was on a wilderness adventure—a cure for troubled youths. They had been out for several days on their survival trip and the victim had become ill. She become too sick to walk and died.

I tried to radio this information to park headquarters, but my handheld radio lacked the range. After a short discussion Bruce decided to return to the plane, take off, and, once up, he would be able to radio back to park headquarters.

I watched from the road as Bruce taxied to the far end of the strip. The plane's engine revved to a roar. Bruce held it with the brake. Dust fogged up, the plane shook, and slowly began its takeoff roll. The field was soft and the plane accelerated slowly, too slowly. Ponderosa pines sixty or seventy feet tall lined the far end of the runway. As the distance between the plane and the trees narrowed, my heart rate increased. An accident was taking place before my eyes. Then the plane came up, skimmed over the ground, but struggled to gain altitude. I could see it was going to be close. In the last seconds, the plane, seeming to sense danger, climbed faster. The tree tops passed just below the tail.

When I was able to speak in a normal voice I called Bruce, "That looked scary from here."

Bruce answered, "It looked scary from here too!" and then he added, "I'm not coming back."

Bruce radioed the situation to headquarters and made the necessary arrangements, but until help arrived, I was on my own. No one attempted to repeat Bruce's daring landing and for vehicles there was no direct route. It took hours for investigators from Kingman, Arizona, to arrive.

It was a long, painful day.

- 30 -

Wilson Ridge

The late afternoon looked and felt like winter. During the early morning hours a swarm of sightseeing airplanes had taken off under clear skies and headed towards the Grand Canyon. But now the blue sky was gone and it was cold, grey and overcast.

I was at home when Dave, the Park Search and Rescue Coordinator, called. He told me Dispatch had received an ELT report. I knew what that meant. Modern commercial aircraft carry a device called an emergency locator transponder, or ELT. In the simplest terms, it is a radio that broadcasts a signal that can be used to locate an aircraft. The device is designed to automatically activate in the event of a crash.

Immediately after Dave's telephone call I drove to Fire Station Four where we kept the SAR (search and rescue) cache. Dave was busy packing ropes, carabineers and anything we might need for a rescue into the big orange packs the SAR team carried. Without stopping his work he explained that the ELT signal seemed to be coming from inside the Park—from the Black Mountains near Mount Wilson.

The Black Mountains are a string of peaks forming a north-south ridgeline like a serrated knife blade a few miles east of the Colorado River. The highest point, Mount Wilson, is a little over 5,000 feet above sea level.

No one had called for the search and rescue team yet. In fact, it was still not clear if there was a reason for the SAR team because it takes time to sort through all the confusion to get to the facts. This sorting was still going on at headquarters, but Dave, our new SAR coordinator, believed in being prepared. When the call came, our all-volunteer team, equipped at their own expense, would be ready.

A few minutes later we received the call. A sightseeing airplane trying to return to Las Vegas after spending the day at Grand Canyon was missing. Along with the pilot there were four visitors from France on board. The ELT signal, we were told, was weak and only gave a vague location. The aircraft could be anywhere within several square miles of rugged wilderness.

There was very little time left before dark. Dave wanted to have at least one team on the ground before sunset. When enough SAR team members arrived at the fire station, we moved out.

The ELT signal was in the Temple Bar District and Bud, the Temple Bar District Ranger, met us where a jeep road turned off the main road. Bud and Dave spread maps out on the hood of the truck and, after a short conference, decided that Bud would establish a command post and Dave would take our searchers up the jeep road to a jumping off point as close to the base of Mount Wilson as possible. From there, three teams would take separate but parallel routes up the mountain to reach the summit ridgeline. From my backseat viewpoint the plan sounded good. I was to lead one of the teams and was anxious to get started.

Because of the rush to get teams in the field, we had left the SAR cache before all the team members had arrived. In fact, other than myself, there were only two others that were a part of the unit. The remainder of our group were rangers from Boulder Beach, Willow Beach, and Temple Bar. Kevin, a ranger from Willow Beach, was an experienced rescuer. The others were all highly motivated but had less experience. Kevin was placed in charge of team one. I had team two and Terry, another SAR leader, had team three.

The three teams marched away from the truck on diverging courses. After a few minutes the ground became much steeper. I picked my way between scrubby brush and loose rocks. When I looked back I was surprised to see how much altitude we had gained, but I could still make out Dave standing in the headlights of his truck.

Our breathing became heavy and labored as we struggled up the rocky ground. In places the slope became so steep we had to scramble using hands and feet. Every fifteen or twenty minutes I would call a halt to rest and get our bearings. The night sky was black; not a star shone. The only light in the world came from our puny headlamps and I couldn't help but imagine an injured person lying out in this darkness scared, in pain, cold, and alone. They would be thinking of family. They would be wondering if anyone knew what had happened and if anyone was coming.

Shortly before midnight, we struggled the last few steps onto the summit. The exertion of the climb had left me wet with sweat and now standing on the ridge I felt the bite of the cold wind. The ground fell away sharply on either side and in the blackness the drops seemed bottomless. I radioed Dave and he instructed us to go south to link up with Kevin's team.

Since doing anything was better than standing there, we walked along the ridge a few hundred yards to the spot where I expected to meet Kevin. The damp, cold wind made standing still downright miserable. I pulled my hood up and turned my back to the elements. Any survivors out there, I thought, would be hard-pressed to endure.

When Kevin and his team joined us we began working south along the ridge. It was painfully clear that unless the plane was within a few feet of the top of the mountain we would never see it. Nevertheless we kept moving. We knew we were all any survivors had going for them.

After several hundred yards Kevin and I called a halt. Because there was little to be gained by continuing on blindly, we sought shelter on the lee side of the ridge at the base of some large boulders. I was hungry and wasted no time in extracting a MRE (meal ready to eat) from my pack. MREs are a sealed plastic pouch, slightly larger than and shaped like a brick. They were developed for the military and while not always tasty, they contained plenty of nourishment.

As I tore open the brown plastic pouch I looked up and saw my teammates just sitting there, looking at me, and not eating. Suddenly

I realized neither of them had anything to eat. I glanced at Kevin and saw that he was the only member of his team with food. But there was enough in the MREs for all of us to have something. I divided my meal, offering Ray and Whalen what I considered the prize—meatballs in tomato sauce. Ray politely declined. Politeness, shyness, manliness, or whateverthe reason for his refusal irritated me. With much more forcefulness, bordering on aggression, I shoved the packet into his hands. This moment would have gone unremembered but for one thing. Years later Ray told me he was a vegetarian and we had a good laugh.

After dinner, such as it was, each man sought the largest boulder he could find for shelter. But after 30 minutes Kevin and I discovered our teammates were dangerously cold, bordering on hypothermia. We concluded it was time to get everyone off the mountain.

The following morning, as soon as there was enough light to take off, the park plane and several private planes began a search. The weather had improved and within minutes of beginning the search wreckage was discovered near the summit.

A U.S. Air Force rescue helicopter from Nellis AFB picked up our SAR teams at Dave's outpost and lifted us to the ridge line just above the crash site. On our way up I sat where I could see the ground and the ridge that had taken hours to climb the night before. I scanned the slopes for sight of the wreck, but saw only rocky outcrops and boulders. Then as the ship banked for its final approach to the ridge I saw it. About a hundred feet below the top of the mountain at the base of a cliffy outcrop was a black smudge. Scattered about the stain were small flecks of shiney litter. At the foot of the smudge was the rear section of the plane. The tail rudder and elevators were all that was identifiable. It was painfully obvious that there were no survivors.

Our team had been within a few hundred yards of the site the night before. After all our work, all our discomfort, our best efforts hadn't mattered. We had been very close, but the passengers had perished before I even walked over to the fire station the afternoon before.

After the initial flush of disappointment I looked around me at the faces in the crowded helicopter. These people, my teammates, had been willing to sacrifice and endure misery to help strangers. These were the kind of men that gave hope to victims and victims' families alike. Without them, without men and women willing to put themselves on the line, where would we be? It mattered very much that these rescuers were strong, trained, dedicated, and willing. It mattered because there would be a next time.

- 31 -

A Very Tough Summer

I shall always remember 1992 as a very tough time. What happened that summer shook my confidence, left me with doubts, and eventually redirected my life. Prior to that summer I had been a rising star, winning awards, accolades, and racking up a file drawer full of "outstanding" performance evaluations.

The first event that shook my confidence began the summer before when a seasonal undercover ranger noticed a pickup truck parked on the shoulder of the Hemenway access road and asked me to investigate. What I found was a highly intoxicated man sitting in the truck. He wasn't driving and because no one had seen him driving and the keys were in his pocket I really did not have a case for driving under the influence. But I did arrest him for public intoxication. When I searched the truck I found two unloaded handguns in cases behind the seat. On the trip to jail the man seemed to be a typical drunk, but he did say one thing I found unusual. He said, "They're out to get me." Still I figured this odd remark was simply the meaningless babble of a drunk.

Several months later, while watching the evening news, Dan Rather launched into the top story about a crazed gunman who drove his pickup truck through the window of a cafeteria in Killen, Texas. He shot and killed twenty-three people before being shot. Because I recognized the name, I called Dispatch to verify that it was the same guy I had arrested.

A short time later, my phone rang and it was the Chief Ranger asking me to come to headquarters right away because the Park

Investigator wanted to talk to me. The Chief's tone of voice implied that I had done something wrong. Before, I had been upset by the deaths of so many innocent people, but now I felt like some kind of suspect, like I had been negligent or had not followed proper procedure when I had arrested this man.

Before I sat down for my interview I asked myself: Did I screw up? Did I miss something? What could I have done differently? The investigator asked me to go over everything. When we were done, I asked him if I was in trouble. He seemed surprised by the question and reassured me that, of course, I couldn't have known what would happen and I had done everything right. I felt better, but nevertheless I couldn't help wondering why my superior had questioned my competence.

A second incident might have ended as a funny story if it weren't for the fact that my chief mentor and immediate boss was not pleased with me.

In the early 1990s, the Grateful Dead, the rock group, began playing concerts in Las Vegas each year and their followers, the Deadheads, would camp at Lake Mead. The first year we didn't know what to expect and were unprepared when hundreds of Deadheads invaded our campgrounds. For three days, each night after the concert, old hippies smoked dope and partied until the wee hours of the morning. Management was not amused.

Before the second year's event, an aggressive plan was formed to maintain control. I was the night shift supervisor and had twenty rangers, game wardens, and highway patrol officers at my command. My task was clear: don't let parties on the beaches and campgrounds get out of control. Checkpoints were set up on the roads entering the park. Rangers were posted at every campground entrance with instructions to block the entrance and turn away the Deadheads as soon as all the campsites were taken.

By 10 p.m. on the first night of the concert all the campgrounds were full and we turned away hundreds of Deadheads. Rangers roamed about on foot and by car, looking for trouble, and seizing the pot smokers' stashes. All went well and by 1 a.m. the campgrounds were quiet and roads deserted. It appeared we had won the day, or night.

I decided to take one final look around the district, and if all was still quiet I would dismiss the shift. As I drove along Lakeshore Road, I saw the glow of a big fire in an unimproved beach area called Saddle Cove. I drove down the short access road and came to a stop at the head of an elevated causeway linking Saddle Island with the shore. From this vantage point I could see down onto the beach.

What I saw was a huge bonfire, 10-15 feet in diameter with flames shooting 20 feet into the air. Around it were hundreds of dancing, singing, drinking, and pot smoking Deadheads. Outside the ring of people were hundreds of parked cars. Earlier I had wondered where the Deadheads had gone after we turned them around at the campground gates. I had assumed that they had left the park. I was wrong.

I summoned the night shift to my location. As I waited for the cavalry to arrive, I studied the scene. The crowd seemed relatively stationary and mellow. It looked like they planned to spend the night. The spot they had chosen was a large, sandy beach and, even though the fire in the center was huge, there was no vegetation near and no danger of the fire spreading.

When reinforcements arrived, we gathered like Custer's 7th overlooking the valley of the Little Big Horn. I sent two scouts, undercover rangers, down to check the place out. On return they reported that there was some drinking and dope smoking, but for the most part the people appeared to pose no danger to either themselves or the park.

My first reaction upon discovering the scene had been to shut the fun down, arrest the violators, and run the rest off. But after looking the situation over, I knew that was a bad idea. If I charged in with my entire shift, the best I could hope for was a few arrests and we would flush a lot of impaired people onto the road. At worst it would be like Little Big Horn and I could create a full-blown riot. After weighing my options I chose to let sleeping dogs lie. I dismissed the shift and we all went home.

The next morning the District Ranger discovered the group camp and he was not at all pleased. He felt I had made a mistake. His approval was important to me and once again I felt that my competence was being questioned.

It was however, what happened on one hot summer day a few weeks later that forever changed me and changed how I felt about rangering. When I arrived at work that day I found the boat crew and land patrol at the harbor launch ramp preparing a near drowning victim for transport to the hospital in Las Vegas. I asked if there was anything I could do to help and one of the rangers asked me to go to South Swimming Beach where the accident had occurred to see if I could locate any witnesses.

I drove slowly down the beach access road past the campground, past the picnic area, out onto the beach which was crowded with hundreds of people. Several rows of parked cars paralleled the packed beach where families, children, singles, and groups splashed in the water and lounged on shore. The only downside to the otherwise typical weekend day was a strong, offshore breeze. The wind blowing out of the south off the land was strong enough to occasionally kick up sand in a stinging spray and send any unattended paper plate, candy wrapper, or beach ball sailing out over the water.

I crept along surveying the scene. Suddenly I was startled by a frantic woman beating on the car's side window. Before I could get the window down she screamed, "There's a baby on a raft being blown out onto the lake." At the same moment, the radio burst out, "430, 700; I have a report of a child on an inflatable raft being blown onto open water off of South Beach."

Immediately I realized that the people on the beach who, from a distance, had looked like they were playing and having fun, were waving and pointing at a tiny form riding on a toy alligator. The inflatable bobbed atop angry waves three or four hundred yards offshore, well beyond the buoys that marked the swimming area. The wind was pushing the toy out faster than any Olympic swimmer could swim. Yet it was apparent from the number of tired Good Samaritans clinging to the buoys that many had tried.

The crowd screamed at me to do something. For an instant I thought about swimming after the toy. But I knew I would never be able to catch up to the toddler. My next thought was to alert the boat that regularly patrolled the water just beyond the buoys. However, the patrol boat was at the Marina where the near downing victim had been delivered to a waiting ambulance. I grabbed the radio mic, called the patrol boat, and told Penny, the boat operator, to get back here fast.

After making the call, the only thing I could do was watch. I needed to keep my eyes focused on the toy so I could direct Penny. Without thinking about possible damage, I jumped on top of my patrol car, where my view was unobstructed.

The baby was now a dark dot upon the angry water. The further out the toy sailed, the larger the waves became. My thoughts screamed in my head, "Hurry, Penny, hurry!" At any moment I knew the waves would capsize the toy. I fixed my eyes on the distant speck, afraid to even blink. My only purpose now was to guide the boat to the rescue. Time slowed to a standstill. My every sense focused to a pinpoint. I no longer heard the crowd. I was aware of nothing around me. I only saw the tiny inflatable toy sliding out to sea.

And then I saw it and felt it. As if in slow motion the toy rose up, one side of the alligator climbed higher and higher, and then over it turned. Its precious cargo spilled into the churning waves. With its burden gone the alligator began a tumbling dance as it fled the scene.

The baby had disappeared and I could see only the angry waves. My thoughts screamed a prayer, "Dear God, no, please don't let this happen."

Then I saw the tall form of the Skipjack patrol boat gallop into view. A long, white wake trailed the boat, emphasizing its speed. Penny had raced from the Marina in less than a minute and a half. Rescue was still possible; we can do this I thought.

Keeping my eyes on the place where I had last seen the baby, I radioed directions: "Straight ahead! More to your starboard! Right there! That's it!" The boat passed the spot then wheeled about and stopped. I saw the deck hand, Diane, pull something from the water. "Got him," Penny called.

"Bring him to me," I shouted over the radio. Every second counted. It would take too long to transport the baby back to the

Marina. Boats weren't allowed in the swimming area but that didn't matter now. Meanwhile, Jim Sanborn had called for Rescue Four, our ambulance, and when it arrived he had stopped it right behind my patrol car. The medic, Renee, was beside me. As the patrol boat raced for shore, I stripped off my gun belt and radio, handed them to Renee and ran into the water. I waded out waist deep and the boat glided up next to me.

Diane passed the tiny, limp body down into my arms. I spun around and ran in the water while at the same time beginning CPR. Pressing on the small chest and puffing life-giving air into his lungs. I ran and leaped up into the ambulance. Jim slammed the doors behind me and Renee called out to the driver, "Go, go."

I laid the baby out on the gurney. His small arms flopped straight out from his side as I continued CPR. Renee began lifesaving efforts. There were no obvious signs of life, yet with each bump in the road the little arms moved up and down. I prayed it was the baby moving his limbs. As I worked I suddenly became aware that there was another person in the vehicle with us. The child's father sat quietly in a corner, his eyes fixed on the boy in wide-eyed terror.

The normal entrance to the Boulder City Hospital emergency room was closed due to construction. We were forced to pull up to the back door, a considerable distance away. Once again I cradled the boy and Renee grabbed my belt helping to propel me down the long corridor. All the while I was doing CPR. I was near my limit. I had been giving the boy all my spare breath for twenty minutes and now this final surge of effort was taking its toll. Like in a childhood dream of trying to escape monsters, I couldn't seem to move my feet much faster than a walk. I wanted to go faster but couldn't.

The emergency room nurse took the child from me. I stepped back and watched as the nurse laid the tiny form on the stark white sheets. Immediately the baby was surrounded by doctors and nurses. There was nothing more I could do.

Renee and I waited around for a while, hoping for good news. But it never came. I had seen death many times, and would see it many more times, but this little man's death hurt more and changed me more than any others. I had watched him die. I had held him in my arms as if he were my own. I had given my all to save him. That night, as I sat in the dark on my back porch, silent tears rolled down my cheeks.

- 32 -

Happy Times

As I drove across the Las Vegas Bay Bridge, as a matter of habit, I looked down at the dirty brown stream that flowed from the Las Vegas water treatment plant to Lake Mead. Technically the water was "clean," but it never looked or smelled clean. However, in spite of the odor, I sometimes saw a few people down in the wash. On this day I saw only a small, white dog.

A few hours later on my return trip, I looked to see if the dog was still there. He was. When I pulled over to check out the situation, I saw the dog was trapped with brown water racing past in front of him and steep cliffs behind and on both sides. The dog was either lost or abandoned. I suspected it was the latter.

I called Jim Sanborn, the new leader of the SAR team, and we planned the rescue which we officially designated a swift water rescue training exercise. With a full rescue team, a canoe, and a long rope we returned to the wash. Jim sat in the canoe and the team floated it on a long rope out into the swift current. He paddled across the stream and scooped up the friendly, little mutt. Then the team hauled him back across and Jim delivered the dog to me. It was a perfectly executed rescue. But what was I going to do now?

Procedure dictated I turn the dog over to animal control. However, I knew if he was not claimed in a week he would be euthanized. That felt wrong. I had to ensure he would be adopted.

The Park Public Information Officer had once told me that people loved rescue and dog stories. So how about a rescued dog story? I took "Lucky" to headquarters and introduced him to the PIO. Soon she had the local media interested and Lucky's story appeared on the local evening news. The very next day the Boulder City Animal Shelter was overwhelmed with calls and Lucky found a new home.

Some time after this dramatic rescue, Jim and I teamed up to play a practical joke on a new member of the SAR team. I really believe a sense of humor is a necessary counter balance to the too-often-serious side of life. From time to time I've livened things up around the office with little practical jokes—like the time I left a page in the copy machine at headquarters with the names of top management along with the whistleblower "hotline" telephone number. Or the more elaborate caper of the phony bomb made from road flares planted in Dave's desk.

The opportunity for a classic prank developed when the seasonal ranger at Shivwits discovered an unknown cave, which held promise of being an undisturbed archaeological site. Since the cave was below the Grand Canyon rim and would be difficult to reach, the archaeologist asked for some climbers from the SAR team to go with her. The entire group would be flown to the area in one of the Air Force's Blackhawk-type helicopters.

On the morning of the trip, Jim and I went to the SAR cache to distribute the necessary gear—ropes, slings, carabineers, and such—into three packs. Because the third and newest member of our team, Andy, wasn't helping us pack the gear, he became the butt of our prank. We thought of it as sort of an initiation. Andy was in the Naval Reserve. He was a physically fit rescue swimmer and inclined to brag about his strength and stamina. As Jim and I filled the packs we decided to add a little weight to Andy's pack. In addition to his share of the load we added some rocks.

Jim's and my packs weighed around forty pounds. Poor Andy's was close to a hundred. He commented at the airport as we were loading up that his pack was heavy. Of course, we called him a wimp.

Arriving at the rim of the Grand Canyon near Shivwits, the helicopter circled looking for a place to land. Below us were rolling piñon and juniper-covered hills. The entire scene glistened under a foot of brilliant white snow. It was beautiful. After a few circles, the helicopter landed in a clearing about a mile away from the rim. I thought the pilot could have found a landing place closer to our destination. But with a wink, the pilot explained that there were no good landing spots any closer.

We shouldered our packs and started out. Andy immediately fell behind. Jim and I reached the rim above the cave and had time to drop our packs and sit down before Andy finally trudged up. As he unshouldered his pack he commented that his pack seemed awfully heavy. We called him panty waist and a cry baby. Then, figuring the joke had gone far enough, I started digging through his rucksack pulling out one fist-size rock after another. At first Andy was mad, but then he realized this was his initiation. He was now part of the team.

But Jim and I weren't the only ones playing a practical joke that day. As we sat resting from our long hike, the helicopter's engine started, the ship lifted off, circled overhead and landed not a hundred yards away.

- 33 -

Clean Up the North Shore

In the spring of 1993, the Las Vegas Wash District and the Boulder Beach District were merged. The new jumbo district was led by Bob McKeever. Donna from Vegas Bay joined the crew. Our backcountry responsibilities doubled, but the difficulty of the job actually tripled or quadrupled. It wasn't just a matter of the territory doubling. The new backcountry was in large measure a war zone. Upper Gypsum, Lower Gypsum, and Government Wash were popular with juveniles seeking to avoid authority, street gangs, and borderline criminals. Rangers, when they dared to venture into these areas, generally patrolled in pairs. It wasn't just for personal protection, but also for the protection of patrol vehicles. Once, while a ranger was away from his car making an arrest, some of the locals pushed his vehicle off a hill and let it roll down into the lake. Another time, while rangers were performing CPR on a drowning victim, hooligans above threw rocks at them just for fun. These areas had gotten so far out of control that rangers no longer proactively patrolled them and only entered to deal with problems: fights, drownings, shots fired, and such.

When Bob McKeever took over, he made it clear that this condition was intolerable. His plan was beautifully simple, we would maintain a presence for as many hours a day as was possible with our meager staff and there would be no Mister Nice-Guy Ranger. Every violation would be dealt with by citation or arrest.

At the end of March when visitation began to climb, Bob's campaign kicked off. The entire backcountry unit was put on the night shift because the yahoos were used to the rangers going home shortly after dark. Night after night we stepped out of the dark into the campfire light and caught juveniles frantically trying to hide their beer and dope.

Upper Gypsum, also known as "the Cliffs," was a favorite place for rowdy, young men to hang out. During the day they would dare one another to jump off the twenty foot high cliffs into the water. Sadly, at least once or twice a year, the results would be a drowning or quadriplegic. At night when they thought they were safe from authority, the partying and drinking would begin.

One typical night early in our campaign, Donna, Jim and I gathered at the head of Upper Gypsum. After discussing our tactics, we moved in. A short way down the arroyo we came to the first party. The three of us quickly rounded up all of the under-age drinkers. Jim and I left Donna to finish writing the citations and we pressed on to the next trouble spot. The second group was camped out on a point overlooking the lake. Once again, with surprise and speed, we caught a number of kids drinking. The group was rounded up and as Jim began issuing tickets I noticed another party near the bottom of the hill. Since Jim had control of the hilltop partiers, I walked down to deal with the third group.

As I eased up to within ten yards of their huge bonfire and remaining outside the firelight, I could see these folks were not juveniles. These were highly intoxicated adults. As I watched, the man standing nearest to me bent over, picked up a sawed-off shotgun and raised the weapon to his chest.

The second I saw the gun coming up, I drew my revolver and jumped sideways. Boom, the shotgun went off sending a round skyward. Time stopped. My senses sharpened; it was as if I could hear his—or was it my?—heartbeat. I was keenly aware of everything. My finger increased pressure on the trigger. In another second, my weapon would discharge. It was kill or be killed.

However, when I shouted, "Ranger, drop the weapon!" the shotgun sprang from his hands. The pressure came off my trigger finger. I ordered everyone onto the ground. Even with the offenders on the ground, this was still a dangerous situation.

That's when I heard the comforting sound of Jim racking his 12-gauge shotgun. He shouted, "I got them covered."

Jim later told me that when he heard the shotgun go off, he figured they had shot me, because he knew I didn't have a long gun with me. No one would have questioned him if he had sought cover until he could determine what had happened, but he had come to my rescue. Of course, I later kidded him, saying that the only reason he hurried down the hill was because he thought he had just heard a supervisory position open up.

However, winning back the North Shore took more than aggressive law enforcement. We also needed to change the ground conditions that aided the bad behavior. Because the superintendent has the authority to make certain local rules and regulations, Bob asked that Upper Gypsum be closed to the possession of alcohol and Lower Gypsum be closed period.

Park superintendents hate controversy and rarely go out on a limb, so we had to make a very strong case for the changes. To help drive home our requests, Bob arranged for me to take the Superintendent and some top staffers on a show-and-tell trip. As we drove through the war zones, I kept up a running commentary. However, what they saw told the real story. Garbage and broken beer bottles were everywhere and the desert was crisscrossed by hundreds of vehicle tracks. Vegetation was beaten back and the soil churned. In the worst places the scene was reminiscent of a battlefield, and in some ways it was.

None of this should have been a surprise, because the Superintendent and the top brass saw the incident reports every day, yet how bad it really was had not registered. But with the evidence before them, the numbers on reports became significant. In short order, regulation changes were made as fast as the system could process them. Things began shifting in our favor.

We kept the pressure up and by early summer it was clear we were winning. Each weekend we had fewer and fewer incidents. We were gaining the upper hand with behavioral problems, but environmental damage was still occurring. Off-road vehicles were literally destroying the fragile desert, where disturbed soil can take decades to recover.

My goal became to keep all vehicles confined to the designated roads. We posted dozens of signs. But as fast as we put the signs up, violators destroyed them—shot them full of holes, ran them over, burned them, or stole them. The public had been allowed for many years to drive pretty much wherever they wanted and now they resisted our attempt to keep them on approved roads.

Then one day an unexpected opportunity occurred. Roy, the park's equipment operator, pulled up next to where I was parked at the top of Gypsum Wash in his road grader and I had an inspiration. Why couldn't Roy blade a deep bar ditch down each side of the road—big enough that a vehicle couldn't cross it? When I mentioned it to Roy, he agreed that it would take care of the off-road vehicle problem, but added he'd need clearance—approval from someone in authority. With yet another inspiration, I held up a handful of papers from my front seat and lied, "Got it right here, Roy."

With that act, I short-circuited the bureaucratic nonsense of obtaining a clearance for the vastly more important need to stop off-road travel.

Following my instructions, Roy dug deep ditches on either side of the road. The trenches were perfect. No vehicle could cross them. I decided to press my luck a bit more and asked him do the same at Government Wash. That was going to be the limit of my renegade work since they were the two worst places and there was no need to draw undue attention to my activities.

Had it ended there, all would have been fine. But it didn't. I went on my days off and Roy, misunderstanding how much work I wanted, went on to grade bar ditches down both sides of Lake Mead Boulevard. Unapproved trenches beside a minor backcountry track would have gone unnoticed, but these same trenches along either side of Lake Mead Boulevard—the main entrance to the park—were much too obvious. They were soon discovered by the Chief of Maintenance and he was not happy.

District Ranger Bob got a call from HQ demanding to know what was going on. Of course, he didn't know anything. But even though he had no knowledge, it was his district and he claimed responsibility. That's when I knew I had to protect Bob as well as answer for my actions.

I immediately telephoned the Superintendent's office. When the Superintendent came on the line I said, "I hear there is going to be a hanging and I'm the guest of honor." Before he could answer, I went on to explain that I, not Bob, was responsible for the ditches. I told him how I tricked Roy and left Bob in the dark. I ended by admitting that I knew better and would accept any discipline he wished to administer without protest or appeal.

I was guilty. Was my action bad enough to be fired or would it be just a few weeks without pay? I knew the system had low tolerance for violations of procedure. It mattered little that my heart was in the right place, or that in time the ditches would prove effective in protecting the desert.

I waited for the Superintendent to pronounce my sentence. After a moment of silence he said, "Chuck, don't ever do that again." With that simple decision, he made me a better ranger and a better leader.

By the end of summer North Shore was no longer a war zone. With Bob's determination and guidance, we had wrestled control of Gypsum and Government Washes away from the riffraff and returned control to the park rangers. Jim, Donna, and I felt proud of a job well done.

- 34 -

Crisis

Crisis—that may be too strong a word—but for some time I had been experiencing dissatisfaction with my career choice. The pressure of intense law enforcement activity in our effort to clean up the Northshore had dredged up feelings that had been buried. There had been times on the worst, hot, busy, summer weekends when I had had butterflies in my stomach prior to going to work because I knew before the shift was over, something bad would happen. Someone would die, someone would suffer a life-threatening injury, or I would be in a fight. I likened my anxiety to what I imagined soldiers feel before going into battle.

I coped by confronting my fears head on, rushing in when trouble occurred. As a consequence, I was first on the scene for more than my fair share of incidents. This rushing in did sometimes get me into unnecessary trouble.

One of those times when I should have waited happened when the dispatcher radioed that two patrons were creating a disturbance at the Lake Mead Marina Bar. I was close by and another ranger, Malcolm, was at the Alan Bible Visitor Center three miles away. I answered that I would handle it and Malcolm said he'd be right down to help. Waiting for Malcolm was the prudent thing to do, but I decided I would slip in through the kitchen, get where I could see the bar area and size up the problem.

When I peeked out the door I saw two big, boisterous drunks. They weren't causing problems at the moment, but I could see that their obnoxious behavior could easily get out of hand. I was just about to ease back into the kitchen and wait for Malcolm when one of the drunks looked up and saw me. Even though he called out to me, I still should have still backed out and waited for help.

Instead I said, "Say guys, you're getting a little loud. There are other people around having dinner."

Their response was something like, "So what ya gonna do about it?" I knew this was going downhill fast and good sense was now taking hold. I started to back out the door to the breezeway. To my dismay they both got up to follow me and that is when I saw that they were huge men. I knew a fight was coming and since I had left my baton in the cruiser I had lost my tactical advantage.

Outside in the breezeway the confrontation began again. I demanded I.D.s. Their answer was, "F... you!" They started to walk past me and the fight was on. It was two against one. But Malcolm arrived in the nick of time. As I was about to go down, one of my adversaries was suddenly jerked backwards and slammed face first into the adjacent wall.

That incident was enough to give me second thoughts. Of course, I should have waited for Malcolm and avoided this close call. But I really never was a law dog. I had chosen rangering based on a flawed belief it would be like John Riffey's world. I had believed that I would protect my park, help people have an enjoyable outdoor experience and when necessary, save lives. The initial dream had never materialized and now, with the newness gone, with the initial challenges met, I was beginning to see this wasn't where I belonged.

Later that summer, Bob McKeever transferred to headquarters and Tim became my new boss. A new leader meant new plans for the district and I needed to know how I would fit in.

One day, shortly after this transfer, when Tim was a captive audience in my patrol vehicle I told him I was thinking of moving on unless I saw a better future in the district. I mentioned my vision of full-time backcountry work. Tim listened, but could not promise me a position that would fulfill my dream. The best he could offer was a suggestion that I should be patient because, "the park has plans for you."

214

I found myself asking: What plans? When? I wanted change now. Based on my belief that being a ranger meant being like John Riffey, I had taken the wrong career path. It was time to correct this mistake. I was ready for a change. But where would I find this new path and where would it take me?

- 35 -

Change

When the Park Maintenance Division announced they were hiring a carpenter apprentice, I studied the job announcement, weighed each word and decided it was the path I had been searching for. It was like a gift from above.

Twenty years before I had chosen rangering without hesitation or doubt because I wanted to follow in Riffey's footsteps. If I actually could have lived as he had lived, it would have been the right choice. Disappointed, I was ready for another career and here, on this paper, was a chance for a do-over. The more I thought about it, the more I knew this was the right path. I wouldn't have to leave the Park Service, which I truly loved. I wouldn't even have to move from Lake Mead, which felt like home. But most importantly, the job felt right. It offered creativity, challenge, variety, and escape from law enforcement or the confines of an office. I welcomed the chance to work with my hands and contemplated with pleasure the idea of maybe someday becoming a craftsman—a builder.

I filled out the application with great care. The questionnaire basically focused on two things—the ability to learn and aptitude for the work. Answering the questions posed no problems, but I felt it wasn't enough. So I enclosed a cover letter attempting to explain why I wanted to give up a promising ranger future to be an apprentice carpenter.

Having made the choice, I worried and waited. Would I make the cut? Would I be chosen for this new position? Finally, in December

1993 I got the call from the Chief of Maintenance offering me the job. Thus, my ranger career of nearly fifteen years came to an end.

Coworkers and friends all gathered together for my goodbye dinner. During the meal it seemed like everyone had a humorous story to tell and laughter filled the room. After the plates were cleared away, the official changing of divisions' ceremony began. I put on a specially prepared uniform and stood at attention before the group. To the steady roll of drums, Tim stepped up and read the charges—desertion. Next, he tore away first my badge, then my shirt sleeves with the arrowhead and finally my Smokey the Bear hat brim. He pulled a toy gun from my holster and replaced it with a toilet plunger. The final disgrace was to issue me a saw horse with a red light and siren attached.

Did I ever look back and question my decision to change careers? Only once and then it was a fleeting feeling. A few weeks after starting my new career I was working on a block wall next to the Las Vegas Bay Ranger Station when the quiet of the morning was pierced by the wail of a siren. I watched as a ranger raced away from the station to some unknown emergency and for just a moment I wanted to go too. I wanted to be on my way to another call. Even though I had hated emergency calls—had answered far more than my fair share—I was like Pavlov's dog, thinking I must go, that this was what I should do.

But as the siren faded into the distance so did my instinctive feeling. I picked up my trowel and went happily back to work.

Epilogue

In January 1994 I entered the Carpenters and Joiners Joint Apprentice Training Center for the beginning of a four-year program. However, I completed the formal training two years ahead of schedule and became a certified journeyman in 1996. I would spend the rest of my Park Service career as a carpenter for Lake Mead National Recreation Area.

Using my newly acquired skills in woodcraft and carpentry I have completely remodeled our home in Boulder City (we no longer live in government housing) and I have added a family room, patio, and workshop to the house. Together, Eileen and I have furnished our living space with antiques. Needless to say our dwelling is a far cry from the mouse-infested house trailer where we began our marriage.

As to rangering, it turns out it wasn't over. For years after I left the Ranger Division, I served as a captain of Engine Four, a wildland fire crew boss, and a SAR team leader. While I spend little time on the water, I continue to train scores of rookie rangers and boating VIPs in basic seamanship. For several years I was the Lake Mead Water SAR coordinator and developed water SAR training programs and procedures that are still used at Lake Mead.

To the very end, while I am not a ranger in title anymore, I am still a ranger in the tradition of my role model John Riffey in heart and spirit.

Chuck Luttrell